Misdem

Beauty Queen Scandals

By

Sally-Ann Fawcett

RB
Rossendale Books

Published by Lulu Enterprises Inc.
3101 Hillsborough Street
Suite 210
Raleigh, NC 27607-5436
United States of America

Published in paperback 2014
Category: Popular Culture
Copyright Sally-Ann Fawcett © 2014
ISBN 978-1-291-90636-3

"I don't think we will ever have a year without a scandal. If we did, it could be boring."

Julia Morley, President Miss World Organisation

Dedication

I dedicate *Misdemeanours* to my dad, John Fawcett, who nurtured and encouraged my love of beauty queens from a tender age, and without whom this book would not have been possible.

Acknowledgements

A heartfelt thank you to everyone who has contributed, advised, cautioned and supported me in the research, writing, editing, and re-editing of this book. I simply couldn't have done it without your patience and enthusiasm.

Special thanks in particular to:
- ❖ Mirrorpix for their permission to reproduce their headline front covers
- ❖ Richard Wendt for his beautiful front cover design - *richardwendtdesign.co.uk*
- ❖ John Kennedy O'Connor, a writer and broadcaster of great talent and skill, for his guidance and inspiration
- ❖ Christopher Long, Journalist, Editor and Foreign Correspondent, for his permission to quote from his in-depth reports on the Pamella Bordes affair - *www.christopherlong.co.uk*.
- ❖ Millymondo for providing some invaluable background information
- ❖ My partner Anthony for his support and exceptional eye for detail
- ❖ My wonderful friends and family for their constant belief in me that never once faltered.

Contents

The Pageants

Miss World

Created by Eric Morley in 1951 as a one-off Bikini Contest for the Festival of Britain. Dubbed "Miss World" by the media, Morley chose to make it an annual event following the start of a rival pageant, Miss Universe, the following year.

Miss Universe

Born 1952 in Long Beach, California, by swimwear manufacturers Pacific Mills. Bought by tycoon Donald Trump in 1996, with NBC as joint partners from 2003. Miss World's biggest pageant rival. The same partners also run and own the Miss USA contest, the winner of which represents the United States in Miss Universe.

Miss International

Started in 1960 when the Miss Universe pageant relocated to Miami. Held in Japan since 1973 and run by the International Culture Association. Seen as the world's third biggest beauty pageant.

Miss United Kingdom

Owned and run by Eric Morley since 1958, to find the British entry to the Miss World contest. The last contest proper was held in 1999 as, following devolution, the four nations of the UK (England, Scotland, Northern Ireland and Wales) take part in Miss World separately. The title of Miss United Kingdom is given to the British contestant with the highest of the judges' scores in Miss World, after the event.

Miss Great Britain

First held in Morecambe in 1945 and run by Lancaster Corporation. Originally the winner went to the Miss World contest but Eric Morley, exasperated at the lack of British success there, created his own heat, Miss United Kingdom, in 1958, to source contestants of a higher quality. Miss Great Britain continued to take place in Morecambe as a stand-alone contest until 1989. The franchise has come under new ownership several times since, but still exists in various forms.

Miss England, Miss Scotland, Miss Wales and Miss Northern Ireland

Separate contests held by the Morleys until handed over to be run by trusted franchisees. Originally the winners qualified for both Miss Universe and Miss United Kingdom contests, but since 1999 have taken part solely in the Miss World finals.

Miss Universe Great Britain

A pageant held since 2004 by a Welsh modelling and PR agency, to find the British representative to Miss Universe. Previously, winners of Eric Morley's contests would take part in Miss Universe.

Miss America

The oldest existing pageant, dating back to 1921, when the first winner was crowned in Atlantic City. Celebrating its 88th year in 2014, the winner does not go forward to any international pageant, but is seen as an American institution that has become a barometer for the changing position of women in society.

Marjorie Wallace

"My advice to the winner? Get a good lawyer"

Marjorie Wallace, Miss World 1973

When Marjorie Wallace's mother said to her, "If you ever have a daughter, you deserve to have one like yourself," it wasn't intended as a compliment.

Of all the thousands of women across the world who have ever attempted to win a beauty contest, the most famous of them all is likely to be the honey-blonde American who is still recalled to this day for her headline-busting behaviour.

Ask anyone with even a modicum of interest in popular affairs and the events of the '70s, and they will immediately remember the beauty from Indianapolis who became the first – and to date, only – Miss World to be stripped of her title.

Even among those who were barely born at the time of her victory, Marjorie Wallace tops the list of the most memorable beauty queens.

Marjorie was the siren who took being Miss World to a new level – that of celebrity in her own right. She was very much her own person, a quality that proved to be her downfall. These days, she'd be a tabloid regular in the mould of Kim Kardashian or Katie Price, with every new beau and every indiscretion a cause for fascination.

And yet rewind forty years and Marji's misdemeanours were more cause for scandal than celebration. It was simply not done back in 1973 to represent a symbol of moral purity and womanhood by sleeping with a footballer and a rock star. Marji was way ahead of her time and the world simply wasn't ready for her – nor were the Miss World organisers, Eric and Julia Morley.

But first, let's go back to that night in November 1973 when Marji took the crown. Much was made of the fact that no American had ever managed to win, and this year's Miss USA was only the second favourite behind Miss Israel.

Yet the moment she appeared on stage at the Royal Albert Hall, she had victory sewn up. Marji glided across the stage and utterly charmed the judges in her interview with the show's long-time host Michael Aspel.

There were few who disagreed that the 19 year old deserved her crown. Yet it was revealed afterwards that there had been a tie for first place between Marji and runner-up Miss Philippines. The chairman of the judges - an American - gave his casting vote to his fellow countrywoman.

Commenting in a newspaper article on her beauty contest success some time later, Marji said, "As long as I was going through with this charade I might as well win. I never felt exploited by the contests because I was using them for my own goals."

It became apparent very soon after her coronation that Marji was in love with the fame and celebrity that her new title brought. As Eric Morley remarked, "It went straight to her head".

Marji was engaged to be married at the time of her win, to Grand Prix racing driver Peter Revson, heir to the Revlon cosmetics empire. "I feel a year as Miss World might test our relationship to the full", she said after her victory. She wasn't wrong.

She met the Welsh singer Tom Jones backstage after one of his concerts and was thrilled when he asked her to appear as a guest in a TV special, to be filmed in Barbados. When Tom was seen giving Marji an on-screen kiss – not contained in the original script – Julia Morley demanded that the controversial shot be edited out. This was the first of many spats between the two headstrong women and they left the island not friends.

As a result of the kiss, rumours were running wild by the time they arrived back to the UK. Marji even offered to ring Tom Jones's wife

Linda to reassure her that there was nothing going on, but concluded that the poor woman was "probably used to this type of thing with his co-stars".

Of all the women Tom had been involved with, he admitted to friends that it was Marji who had got him hooked. "This one could really get to me," he reportedly told them.

Jackie Collins later based one of her bestselling 'bonkbuster' novels, *Lovers & Gamblers*, on the relationship between Tom and Marji, even including a cameo role in the story for long-suffering Linda and their young son.

Marji loved life and she loved men, and she flirted her way through those first months of her reign, charming and infuriating the Morleys in equal measure.

Eddie Crozier, nephew of Julia Morley and an official of the Mecca Organisation, owners of the Miss World contest, recalled a car journey he took with Marji and three male companions. She turned to them, eyes glinting, and asked, "Who is going to ball me out tonight?" She wasn't impressed when Eddie told her that sex wasn't on the agenda that evening.

She insisted that she'd never heard of George Best before she was invited to make an appearance at Slack Alice, the nightclub he owned in Manchester. For his part, the soccer legend was instantly besotted and invited her to Tramp nightclub in London as soon as he could get near her.

The love affair lasted two days. Marji maintains that George flew into a jealous rage when she had to go the BBC to record more of the Tom Jones show, and that after that episode she never saw him again. "I could not believe that any man could behave as childishly as George did," she said at the time.

In his own memoirs, George doesn't speak too highly of Marji and dismisses the relationship lightly.

A magazine ran a story that Marji had given Best three out of ten for performance, while he was said to have retorted, "That's three more than she got".

The fallout from her brief, but very public, liaison with Best was spectacular. She accused him of stealing a fur coat and valuables from her apartment in London, and he was arrested before being released without charge.

The Morleys were mindful of the bad publicity being wreaked on the Miss World brand. Eric invited her to their house in Dulwich to, in his own words, "talk her out of seeing George Best or Tom Jones again."

Marji apologised, promised to sever all contact with the two men – and headed straight to a London hotel for a rendezvous with Tom Jones.

She flew back to the States for a break with fiancé Peter Revson, but upon her return clashed again with Julia over her official engagements, and the die was cast.

Her next meeting with Eric Morley would prove to be her last as Miss World. She was summoned to his office and sacked. Said Eric at the time: "I asked whether she thought we had been fair in view of all the circumstances and she said that she did. She showed no emotion and there were no tears".

The crown was never offered to the runner-up, Miss Philippines. "Now there is no Miss World," Eric confirmed to the press. "No-one will take over the title until the contest is run again in November."

"We do not expect Miss World to live like an angel," said Julia, "None of us is infallible. But it is essential that she should act with decorum.

We accept that she has a personal life – as long as it remains personal."

During Marji's brief reign, she had earned £15,000 from her £500-a-time public appearances, and stood to lose an estimated £50,000 due to its premature ending.

She told the *Daily Express* that there has been no quarrel between her and the Morleys. "I gave up my title purely because of the terrible rumours that have dogged me. I'm really a sweet girl at heart."

Thirty years later, Julia Morley appeared to deny that the dismissal was anything to do with Marji's amorous adventures. In a 2004 interview with *The Times*, she recalled, "The only reason Marjorie was sacked, and quite rightly, was because she had been given so many chances. She was hysterically funny and lovely but she had a big modelling engagement in Paris and other places and she wouldn't get up. Boyfriends had nothing to do with it. I think it is very healthy for a girl to have a boyfriend and a happy social life."

Marji once again returned to the States but her biggest heartache lay ahead. Just two weeks after losing her Miss World title, she was on her way to join Peter Revson for a race in South Africa when she heard the news that he had been killed on a practice lap.

Despite an ill-timed reunion with Tom Jones in Las Vegas not long afterwards, he took the decision to end the affair after pressure from his humiliated wife.

The combination of the stress, grief and loss of the past year was unbearable, and Marji fell into a deep depression. Three months later she took an overdose of sleeping pills. She was rushed to hospital in a coma and was on the critical list for several days, but always denied that she had been trying to commit suicide.

Happily, the ever-optimistic Marjorie bounced back to good health and to her love of publicity. She pointedly flew into London to coincide with a reunion of former Miss World winners to mark the event's Silver Jubilee in 1975 – to which she was not invited.

"My advice to the winner is to get a good lawyer", she said bitterly. "Otherwise she will end up being used as a pawn in a game, which was what happened to me. I was exploited."

She was later linked in a string of romances, including one with the tennis star Jimmy Connors, whom she lured away from fiancée Chris Evert in a love-match that delighted and fascinated the media.

Marji also became a household name back home, for a period hosting both *Good Morning Los Angeles* and *Entertainment Tonight.*

She finally settled down and married multi-millionaire film financier Michael Kline in 1978. The marriage, and a further brief nuptial, was not to last, but Hollywood columnist James Bacon who attended the wedding of her son Adam in 2005 was delighted to report that Marji "still has that spectacular Miss World figure".

In a lasting tribute to the most unforgettable beauty queen of her era, her character appeared in a musical, *Dancing Shoes*, based on the life of ex paramour George Best. It premiered in Belfast in the summer of 2010, with blonde actress Alana Kerr immortalising Marji on stage forever.

When her old flame, now Sir Tom Jones, landed a role as a judge on the BBC's prestigious talent competition *The Voice* in 2012, Marji told the *Mirror* that they were still in touch.

Marjorie, now 61, said: "He is very happy to be doing it and I told him if it was as good as the American version, it will be a huge hit.

"We stayed friends and we are often in touch. I wouldn't want to rehash our relationship as it was so long ago and I have no interest in doing that.

"But it is great to speak to him on the telephone once in a while. I always follow his career and I am really pleased he is going to be coaching up-and-coming singers. He has such a beautiful voice."

Helen Morgan

"I was portrayed as this immoral Jezebel"

Helen Morgan, Miss World 1974

Possibly the second most infamous beauty queen of all time immediately followed Marjorie Wallace's curtailed reign, and turned the mid-'70s into Mecca's worst nightmare.

At the time, though, Helen Elizabeth Morgan may well have benefited from Mecca's relaxation of the morals that stripped Marjorie Wallace of her title.

"Nobody expects Miss World these days to be a blue-eyed virgin", sniffed Julia Morley in response to accusations that, following the American's sacking, the organisation was small-minded and stuffy.

So when Helen revealed, days after winning the Miss UK contest in 1974, that she was an unmarried mother, Mecca bent over backwards to accommodate her.

In 1974, there was no rule to bar women with children from entering the contest. The Morleys had brought in a clause in 1958 to preclude married women, but hadn't had the forethought to take it one step further. As Eric Morley said to the press at the time of the 'unmarried rule' – "Husbands who allow their wives to go in for beauty contests need their heads testing".

Helen, a former bank clerk from Barry, was enjoying a stellar career as a beauty queen. Drafted in to the Miss Cardiff contest to make up the numbers, Helen scooped both that and the Miss Wales titles, going on to finish second in the Miss Universe contest that summer. She strolled to the Miss United Kingdom finals as the obvious winner.

It was a junior reporter back in Wales, Tim Richards, who first realised he had a scoop on his hands when he went to visit Helen at home, days after she had been crowned Miss UK. He noticed an abundance of nappies all over the house and Helen openly admitted she was a single mum to son Richard. "I'm not married, but I'm not ashamed," she said. "I'm proud of my baby".

Tim's story made a huge front page splash not just in the UK, but all over the world.

But the Morleys were adamant that they weren't about to judge her. It didn't matter at all, they said, that Helen had an 18 month old son, from a relationship with her boyfriend, boutique owner Christopher Clode. There was no question of her not taking part in the Miss World contest.

So Helen proceeded to the 1974 finals as hot favourite, with the backing of the Morleys. But as soon as the crown rested on her auburn locks, the first rumblings of discontent began gathering.

Even before she had had a chance to leave the throne on stage, the reporters and photographers had gathered round her like vultures. "Where's your son?", shouted one, thrusting a microphone in her face. "Is he here?"

"Her son has nothing to do with it!", barked Julia Morley, who was trying to control the media scrum.

But of course he had everything to do with it. The more strict Catholic countries immediately denounced Helen's victory as a "moral disgrace", while many contestants believed it was a fix for her to win.

Miss Spain declared to reporters that she believed Helen had only won because of her "condition", while Miss Colombia called the organisation "two faced", for sacking last year's winner due to morals, then crowning a single mother just twelve months later.

Said Miss Venezuela: "In my country, a girl who has a baby without being married is regarded as a bad girl, not pure and undefiled as we are led to believe Miss World should be."

Tony Palmer's groundbreaking 1974 documentary, *The World of Miss World*, followed the build-up to the contest, and uncovered a hotbed of bitterness after the crowning ceremony. "Did you hear the uproar backstage when she won?" Miss Jersey was seen saying to the cameras. "Everyone is very, very upset".

A majority of contestants felt that runner-up Miss South Africa should've won. Despite four out of the nine judges placing her first – one short of an automatic majority - Anneline Kriel lost to Helen by just one point.

Only one of the nine judges – singer and fellow Welshwoman Shirley Bassey – placed Helen first. But Helen received five second places, compared to just one for Anneline.

Helen's situation was unique to the Morleys. As Julia said, "One does not visualise that in the progress of time we have a different society with fresh problems".

Concerned with the negative publicity flying round so soon after Helen's crowning, Julia Morley called an emergency meeting. If Helen resigned that night, the Morleys offered, she could keep half the guaranteed earnings the winner would make over the coming year.

But Helen was adamant that she wouldn't resign. "I couldn't see that I had done anything so terribly wrong", she explained.

The Morleys had no choice but to back her. "This is 1974," stormed Julia, to the baying press corps. "Why shouldn't unmarried mothers have the same chance as anyone else?"

The strain on Helen's face clearly showed during interviews in the first tumultuous days of her reign. "I have to work to support my son," she pleaded, "Why not work as Miss World?" She added, "This is a beauty contest, not one of morals. If they want to test the girls to see if they are virgins, I'm sure they would have no entrants."

Three days after her crowning, a former Cardiff nightclub manager named Raymond Lovegrove emerged from the woodwork. He'd had a fling with Helen, he said, adding that, "She always insisted on going home to her boyfriend every night." Now his wife Linda was threatening to sue him for divorce, naming Helen as co-respondent.

This new revelation resulted in yet more frenzied press attention wherever she went and, for Helen, it was the final straw.

Recalling those final days in an interview with the *Sunday Mirror* in 1998, she said, "I thought, 'Hang on, I've got a son and a family I love very much. Do I want my private life raked over every day and to see them hurt?' So I resigned."

At the time of the divorce story breaking, Helen was in a hotel in Carlisle for her first engagement as Miss World, and was seen in the foyer in tears. She made a telephone call to Julia Morley offering her resignation before leaving through a fire exit door and boarding a sleeper train from Newcastle to London Kings Cross

Eric Morley told the *Express*, "This decision on her part has nothing to do with the baby. It is purely and simply to do with the divorce case.

"Helen was very upset. She told my wife that she felt she should resign, as there was something she hadn't told us."

Her typed statement read, "I believe the rumours being circulated about me would have an undesirable and distressing affect upon my son and family. My child's welfare is, as it is to every mother, of paramount importance to me—far more important than being Miss World.

"I would have deeply liked to have continued as Miss World. It is something every girl reaches for."

The day after Helen's resignation, the *Daily Mirror* ran an interview with Raymond Lovegrove's wife, where she revealed that the true father of baby Richard was not Christopher Clode, as originally reported, but her husband.

Linda found a photograph of Helen and a baby in Raymond's wallet. "He admitted before he walked out that he was the father of Helen's child," she said.

Raymond himself confirmed that this was the case. "When Helen was pregnant, she told me I was the father," he said. "When Richard was born she used to bring him to me and say to the baby, 'Come and see your daddy'.

"She is denying that we had a love affair but before she won a beauty contest I was planning to leave my wife and marry Helen. I was surprised when the papers said that Chris Clode was the father.

"I am surprised that Helen has denied me, but I am willing to take a blood test to prove I am the father."

Helen dismissed the Lovegrove's accusations completely. "I know that Ray Lovegrove is claiming to be the father of my baby. Nothing could be further from the truth." She added. "I don't deny that I know him, but as for ever having gone to bed with him – anyone who suggests that is either dreaming or telling lies."

Runner-up Anneline Kriel, Miss South Africa, inherited the crown. "I'm sorry that I should have to win it in this way," she told the press, "but I have no hesitation in accepting. It is a great honour for me."

Her own reign wasn't without drama, however. Convinced she was being treated as second best to Helen – who was allowed to keep her Miss United Kingdom title and ensuing duties - she deemed her Miss World role as "boring" and threatened to crown her successor wearing jeans. She was also – as the white face of apartheid South Africa – made less than welcome in many countries across the world.

Helen forfeited the prize money that would've gone such a long way towards bringing up her son, and instead she sold her story to a Sunday tabloid, complete with specially posed topless shots. As she said at the time, "Now if anybody asks me what I look like naked, I can just show them these pictures".

The endless publicity surrounding Helen's unfolding story ensured she had the busiest and most successful year of any Miss UK titleholder, finding herself in far greater demand than the woman who succeeded her as Miss World.

She and Chris Clode drifted apart, and in 1978 Helen went on a blind date with businessman Ronny Lamb. They married in 1982, living first in Surrey before moving abroad. That controversial baby son Richard turned 40 in 2013, and the couple have two more adult children, Ben and Poppy.

In the 1998 interview, Helen said, "I'm indifferent to Miss World now. I wouldn't stay home to watch it on TV, but if I was sitting down and it was on, I'd probably watch to see what it was like.

"Whoever wins will probably find it difficult. The press will always be more interested in a scandal than a squeaky-clean winner who just smiles and waves and does all the right things."

Interviewed by the *Daily Mail* in 2000, just before the 50th anniversary of the Miss World contest, Helen reflected on just how stressful the period had been for her.

"The most upsetting aspect was that I was portrayed as this immoral Jezebel," she said. "No-one knew the real circumstances. Things had been awkward at home after my parents had been through a very painful divorce when I was 17. I felt I had no option but to leave and move in with Chris, who I'd been dating for a year.

"Then I fell pregnant. It wasn't planned, but I never even contemplated an abortion."

Reflecting upon her decision to resign as Miss World, she said, "I could've stayed on. The public gave me so much support. I look back and realise I could've stayed and made a go of it."

In what was seen in pageant circles as a huge coup, a Cardiff model agency managed to track down Wales's most famous daughter to her home in Spain, and invited her as a special guest and judge to the Miss Wales 2004 finals, to mark thirty years since her own victory.

The rapturous reception Helen received and the media attention her return warranted is testimony to her enduring appeal as Britain's most famous – and endearing - beauty queen.

And for Helen, there was one last victory. In 2005, *WM Magazine* readers voted her among the top 50 sexiest women in Wales. At the age of 53, this was one accolade she had no intention of handing over.

Eric & Julia Morley

"We do have our fair share of knockers"

Julia Morley, President Miss World Organisation

One throwaway remark lead to the creation of one of the most popular, derided, controversial, and debated television shows in history: Miss World.

"My man Morley will come up with something".

It was 1951 and the scene was the offices of Mecca, at that time a small catering and leisure group. Its managing director, Group Captain Pickard, had received a call from Squadron Leader Phipps, who was in charge of public relations for the Festival of Britain.

Phipps needed ideas from Pickard as to how best they could add glamour and razzmatazz to the proceedings. And that's how Pickard put forward his publicity sales manager, one Eric Douglas Morley.

Morley had already made his mark in the Mecca organisation by creating a TV format to showcase their ever increasing franchise of dance halls via *Come Dancing*, the BBC's longest running TV entertainment show (a brand name now stronger than ever as *Strictly Come Dancing*) in 1949. He later also introduced commercial bingo to the UK in 1961.

But his piece de resistance was in rising to Group Captain Pickard's challenge and coming up with the idea of a contest of 'international bathing beauties'. Twenty-three bikini-clad girls took part and the publicity and controversy over such a daring move was huge. The prize money was vast for those days too - £1,000 going to the winner, Sweden's Kiki Haakonson.

The bikini contest, named 'Miss World' by the popular press, was organised as a one-off, but a year later, an American organisation started a pageant they called Miss Universe. Eric vowed to carry on with his contest, reasoning that, while he had said "World", and they had topped that by saying "Universe", they could never say that they were the first.

Eric Morley was born in 1918, and had an inauspicious start in life. His father died when he was a baby, and his mother and stepfather both died of TB when he was 11. He was sent as an orphan to a Royal Navy training ship and five years later he played French Horn in the Royal Fusiliers.

His talent for combining entertainment and entrepreneurial flair was honed whilst a captain in the Army during the Second World War. He organised the entertainment for the troops, and made his first money by selling squares of toffee for profit.

Back in civvy street, Eric joined Mecca and the rest, as they say, is history and, indeed, often hysterics. By 1971 he was Chairman and Managing Director of Mecca, and under his watch it became the biggest entertainment and leisure company in Britain.

When the group was taken over by Grand Metropolitan Hotels in 1978, Eric was forced out, but he took Miss World with him and the Miss World Organisation was born.

An ardent Tory and admirer of Margaret Thatcher – he vowed that he would do anything for her - he stood as Conservative candidate in Dulwich twice in the '70s and lost on both occasions.

Julia Pritchard was a trained nurse and model when she met Eric in one of Mecca's dance halls, and they married in 1960. She concentrated on raising a family and only became involved in the organisation of the Miss World contest in 1969.

PICTURES BY PETER SHIRLEY

Eric and Julia had very different ideas as to how the contest should be perceived. He was the traditionalist, she the modernist. It was Julia who insisted in the '90s that Miss World should be thereafter termed a 'pageant' as opposed to remaining a 'contest'. Eric was very much against the idea; he said it was too American, too fancy, not British enough.

Eric called them 'girls', Julia called them 'women'.

Eric's reaction to the 'flour bombs and feminists' incidents, mentioned in later chapters, was one of unmitigated glee that the contest was still able to attract so much strength of opinion and publicity, and proof to him of its enduring popularity. His wife's reaction was, according to Julia herself in an interview with *The Observer* in 2001, to request a meeting with the protesters, to see if she could take on their ideas.

Julia has invariably been quoted as a self confessed 'tough bitch' as well as a 'mother hen', depending on whom she was dealing with at the time. When she took over the contest after her husband's sudden death in 2000, she made no apology for trying to modernise the contest and admitted publicly in *The Observer* interview a year later that although she had "enormous respect" for her husband's wisdom, their aims had always differed.

She had already dreamed up the *Beauty with a Purpose* scheme in the '70s, the charity brand for Miss World which has been cited as having raised over $250m for charities around the world so far. She had banned the reporting of the girls' vital statistics in the '80s, and over the years vicariously arranged annual 'themes' for the show, including global warming, children and AIDS.

In an interview with the *Express* in 1978, Julia admitted she was jealous of her husband being around the Miss World girls. "I've always been jealous," she said. "If you'd been pregnant as many times as I have and stood there while gorgeous girls brushed by your bulge, you'd be possessive."

One of her particular challenges was with TV personality Michael Aspel, who hosted the show on behalf of the BBC on and off for fifteen years until 1974. Julia told *The Observer*, "I thought it was pretty awful to see women standing there with practically nothing on, with old Aspel saying, 'What did you eat for breakfast?' - it was so stupid."

The chaperones – multi-lingual women employed to look after the contestants for the duration of the event - didn't think much of him either. One of them revealed that he was all smiles for the camera, but off stage he was "smug and supercilious".

In 1974, Julia publicly blamed Aspel for making the girls look stupid. He retaliated by asking that year's finalists such convoluted and complicated questions that they were unable to answer them. He quit straight after the show.

In a famous and oft-repeated quote, Julia said, "The Miss World contest is still going strong, although we do have our fair share of knockers".

Eric and Julia raised four sons but tragically lost an adopted daughter, Kathryn, in 1985. The 17 year old had suffered from a disease of the nervous system since the age of four, and she was taken gravely ill during the live telecast of the Miss World contest. According to press reports at the time, Julia just had time to hand out the trophies to the winners before slipping away to say a final goodbye to her child.

Julia later said how blessed the family had been to have her, a short, but still a very precious, life.

The couple's oldest son Julian was involved in the running of the Miss World contest for many years and could be seen annually placing the tiaras onto the heads of the runners-up. He also dated Miss World 1980 Kimberley Santos for a while.

Third son Stephen was sentenced to 15 months in jail in 1986 for theft from a client while working for Allied Hambro and during his court case accusations of his father's 'bullying nature' towards him emerged. The *Glasgow Herald* reported that the court heard how Stephen had been made to feel 'inadequate' among such a powerful family dynasty.

Stephen, now calling himself Stephen Douglas, is now Events Manager of the Miss World Organisation and has co-hosted several Miss World finals, while his brother John, the youngest son, sits on the board of an internet technology firm.

Second son, Michael, was accused by gay rights activist Peter Tatchell of assault in 1999. Michael, at the time one of Michael Portillo's minders, allegedly knocked Tatchell to the ground during a heated exchange with the MP over gay equality in an incident that was filmed and subsequently broadcast on Channel 4. The police declined to take matters further.

Eric and Julia Morley themselves were not without controversy on a personal level. Julia's alleged five-year affair with a Guatemalan diplomat, Hector Rosales, was exposed in 1985, while a 32 year woman called Yvonne Smith sold her story in 1989 to *The Sunday People,* telling in great detail of her "office romps" with Eric that continued over a ten-year period.

Julia now shares her home in Dulwich with Grant Harris, a 67 year old former gynaecologist. *The Independent* reported on the court case in 1998 in which Harris was given a six year jail sentence after being found guilty of battering his wife with a hammer before throwing her to her death from their bedroom window.

When questioned by the *Daily Mail* in April 2010 about their relationship, Harris insisted that they were just long-standing friends - indeed, Julia had acted as a character witness at the Old Bailey during his trial - and that his role now was as her odd job man and gardener, while living in his own separate area of the property.

The Miss World contest, for all its vilification, is in many ways an important social document. Whether accidentally or not, it has chartered the course of feminism, apartheid, anti-fur, AIDs, hunger, and poverty.

Eric had many detractors – he never received an honour of any description in recognition of his business and funding raising achievements – but he had many admirers and friends in the show business world too, all of whom made fulsome tributes upon his death.

In its heyday, the Miss World contest was quite simply massive, in a way that TV audiences today, with hundreds of channels to choose from, can't comprehend unless it's a crucial World Cup match, a Royal wedding or funeral, or a talent show finale.

According to research by the British Film Institute, the Miss World shows of 1967 and 1970 share the accolade of being the 17th most watched TV shows *of all time*, with 23.76m viewers (at that time, nearly half the population of the country).

Every great show has its catchphrase, and when Eric took to the microphone to say that he would announce the results "in reverse order", it stuck, and the term has been absorbed into the English language.

The BBC had televised the contest since 1959, but lost the right to screen it in 1979, when it was outbid by Thames Television, who snapped it up for £750,000. The BBC showed its last ever beauty contest – Miss Great Britain – in 1985, before bowing to political correctness.

ITV carried the Miss World mantle until it became plain that viewing figures were beyond resuscitation, and it, too, decided enough was enough, reviving the show briefly in 2001 and 2004 before dropping its option.

From then on, Miss World had to go where the natives were more receptive, and this generally meant the third world, where winning represented the same glory and opportunity as it used to in '60s Britain before the flour bombers moved in. Eric never quite got over the ignominy of being hounded out of his own country and spurned by mainstream British TV. He remained indignant to the end that the British public was being denied access to the show because, as he said during a TV documentary, "the poor taxi driver can't afford satellite TV".

Viewing figures across the world, though, continued to climb – an audience reach of 1 billion was the last estimate, and it is still to this day one of the most watched single annual events in the world, having attracted a record 128 countries or territories to take part in the contest at least once.

The 21st century has seen China and South Africa become Miss World's shared spiritual home, with the odd detour to the Seychelles, Poland, Nigeria and Indonesia. Miss World remains a restless soul, with only its 60th anniversary show in 2011 being held in London for a one-off celebration.

Eric himself at least had the satisfaction of seeing his much-loved baby return to British television before his death. Channel 5 was a fledging broadcaster in 1998 and won the bid to telecast the show from the contest's then temporary home in the Seychelles, and again the following year when it was staged at London's Olympia. Was this what Eric had worked and plotted and prayed for? Miss World back in Britain, back on mainstream British TV?

Channel 5 was very happy with its viewing figures of two million, and had one more year of its contract to screen the contest left to run (before dropping it for reasons of "outdated sexism"). This final show coincided with the 50th anniversary of Miss World in 2000. For its Golden Jubilee, the Millennium Dome had been booked, chat show host Jerry Springer signed up, and a record number of contestants were on their way.

The press naturally leapt on the irony of a white elephant such as the ill-fated Dome hosting the anniversary show of a spectacle they considered a relic of a chauvinistic age, but the Dome's chief executive, Pierre-Yves Gerrbeau, summed it up by pointing out that they were both controversial, yet both fighting back.

For Eric, it was to be his last fight. Two weeks before the contest, amid frenzied preparations, he complained of a severe headache and of being unable to see properly. He was taken to hospital where he died of a heart attack.

A grief-stricken Julia was left to ensure that the anniversary show went on, and she bravely took her late husband's place in announcing the results in reverse order. It was an emotional show, but at the very least it meant a tribute to Eric Morley was seen on British TV, in a British venue, fifty years to the day of the inception of the idea that germinated as a result of that call from Sq Leader Phipps.

Julia's tribute to him all those years later said it all. "Eric", she said, "was honest and funny, with a great sense of humour. Yes, he was brash, and no, he didn't have an Oxford accent. But he cared about everyone he worked with, and if you were in trouble, he was ace".

Mary Leona Gage

"There is no way this could have a happy ending, is there?"

Mary Leona Gage, Miss USA 1957

Scandals in the beauty queen world are nothing new, nor have they particularly evolved as time has moved on. To judge the static nature of what is deemed unacceptable in the beauty queen world, one has to look at the oldest scandal on record and then compare it to the dethroning of far more recent winners for being mothers. Being a beauty queen with children back in 1957 was seen as nothing short of outrageous; it seems little has changed.

The world of beauty pageants has had winners who have turned out to be married, and those who were discovered to have children, but we have to go right back to 1957 to find a beauty queen who could claim both.

In 1957, America was buzzing. Eisenhower was President, *Peyton Place* was the movie of the year, and Elvis Presley ruled the airwaves.

Mary Leona Gage – known simply as Leona – was the Miss USA winner who was subsequently discovered to be married with two children. She was sacked the next day, yet went on to achieve celebrity status in both TV and the movies.

That is the potted version of Leona's story. But in a harrowing interview with the *Baltimore Sun* newspaper in 2005, nearly fifty years later, Leona revealed the less sanitized version of her chequered past and how she was queen for just one day.

According to her self-expose she was pursued, at the age of 13, by an older man, Gene Norris Ennis, who left her pregnant when he returned to his air force duties.

In an attempt to soften the blow for her parents, she eloped with a volunteer groom, airman Edward Thacker, and married him just before she gave birth to Ennis's baby. Her horrified Baptist mother insisted that that marriage be annulled and Leona was sent to live with an aunt until the baby was born.

"To my mother, that was the biggest scandal there could be," she said.

Gene Norris Ennis returned to face the music and he and Leona were married in 1953. By the time Leona was 16, she had had a second child, but neither she nor her 24 year old husband were happy in the marriage.

The drudgery of her daily life compelled the young Mrs Ennis to seek an escape route and, close to a breakdown, she found a job in a shop as a distraction. There she met model and beauty queen, Barbara Mewshew, who inspired her to try her luck following a similar route.

"Leona wanted something of out of life," Barbara told the *Baltimore Sun* in 2005, "and her husband was a real jerk".

Leona joined a modelling agency and put her name forward for the local Miss Maryland beauty pageant, despite knowing she was contravening the rules by being married with children.

In an interview with the *LA Times*, Leona insists she told the Maryland agency from the outset that she was in breach of the regulations. "They told me to forget that I had told them I was married, and to keep my mouth shut".

However the agency insisted that they were never aware of her true status.

As Leona told the press of how she and her cousin had together saved $54 to buy an evening gown for the Miss Maryland pageant, which she won, they dubbed it a 'Cinderella story'. She'd managed to borrow a gown for the Miss USA final and now here she was: the winner, queen of the USA.

She wasn't interested in marriage, she said, she really wanted a career in the movies. "I'm not marrying until I'm 26", she told the *Los Angeles Times*.

She left for Long Beach, California, for the Miss Universe pageant immediately after being crowned Miss USA, and the rumours began to circulate among pageant officials that Leona was married. Her mother in law was suspected as being the source of the gossip, but her son insisted upon her innocence.

The *Los Angeles Times* gained entrance backstage to ask Leona if these rumours were true. She reacted with hysterics and had to be calmed by pageant officials. For the rest of the judging, she was given her own personal security guards and nobody was allowed anywhere near her.

With the preliminary judging over, Leona disappeared to her changing room, and when she emerged she could only wail, "They said they'd get me!" before being led away by the officials.

When confronted by the *Chicago Daily Tribune*, Gene Norris Ennis denied the accusations being levelled at this wife, before adding, "I don't want to get involved in all this".

The next day was the Grand Final of the Miss Universe pageant, and, according to the *Chicago Daily Tribune*, the day that Leona, having repeatedly denied any knowledge of Ennis, decided to come clean.

The paper reported: "After a night of sleeplessness and weeping, Miss Gage admitted her marriage to the organisers."

Leona also admitted that she had two children and had lied about her age. She was, she confessed, only 18 - not the 21 year old she had portrayed herself as being.

The organisers moved swiftly to remove the Miss USA crown she had worn for just one day, and in the proceeding press conference a terrified Leona explained why she had broken the rules. "We needed money badly in Maryland. We owe a lot of bills. My children need clothes."

For his part, husband Ennis told reporters, "I have no objection to her career as long as my children are properly taken care for and they are very well taken care of".

He did, however, strenuously deny Leona's assertions that they were in financial difficulty. "A glance at my wife will convince you she's not starving to death," he added wryly.

As a result of this widely-publicised story, Leona's money problems – whether real or imagined – were solved almost overnight. Offers poured in for movie parts and she appeared on TV chat shows across the country, including the *Ed Sullivan Show*, who said, "What the hell is wrong with motherhood? I want her on my show". Her appearance drew its biggest audience yet.

She relocated to Las Vegas and signed a contract to perform as a showgirl at the Hotel Tropicana. She divorced Ennis and lived in a trailer with her two sons. After briefly dating Frank Sinatra, Leona produced a third son during a short-lived marriage to a dancer.

She moved to Hollywood and married her fourth husband, a screenwriter, and gave birth to her first daughter.

The marriage lasted three years, during which time Leona won small acting roles and at one stage appeared on screen with Racquel Welch. She also firmly established herself on the Hollywood party scene.

She divorced her latest husband in 1964 and life took a downturn for Leona. She lost custody temporarily of her children after concerns that her drug-taking and partying were spiralling out of control. She attempted suicide after taking an overdose of pills and trying to drown herself in the ocean and as a result was hospitalised in a state mental facility for seven weeks.

Leona made her last movie in 1965. It was a box-office flop and, with offers of work drying up, was reduced to working in burlesque clubs, her three year old daughter in tow. The '70s and '80s saw two more husbands and one more son, and she turned to mainstream jobs to pay the rent, including training as a hairdresser.

She contacted Hollywood gossip columnist James Bacon to try and help locate her sons, but the move backfired when he cruelly wrote an article calling her a "plaintive and pleading has-been". It was yet another slap in the face.

During the last year of her life she lived alone in California, requiring a permanent oxygen tank after being diagnosed with chronic pulmonary disease – "It's my jet fuel", she joked.

Two of her five children predeceased her and the other three kept only in sporadic contact before her death in October 2010, at the age of 71.

Her friend Jan Shepard saw Leona very much as the victim. "I don't blame her, I blame the people around her. They used her her entire life. She was naive enough to do things she shouldn't have done, then she got in with the wrong people.

Leona's son Robert Kaminer told the *LA Times on Saturday* of his mother's difficulty in life after losing her title. "When you're 18 years old and you're the most beautiful girl in the room … and then you're 50 and you're on oxygen and you haven't taken the time to develop yourself in other areas, what are you left with?" he said.

In a poignant interview with the *Baltimore Sun* newspaper in 2005, Leona said, "There really is no way this could have a happy ending is there? I was never crazy. I did have a nervous breakdown, but even a dog, if you take away her whole litter of puppies, will get depressed."

Leona still watched the Miss USA pageant, never missed it. "If I wanted to put the real make-up on, I could still look darn good", she smiled.

Marina Papaelia

"I theenk she steenk!"

Marina Papaelia, Miss Egypt 1953

B ad losers are a fact of life in the beauty queen world. Those looks of delight, the hearty applause and the air kisses directed at the winning contestant are very much from the same school which trains the losers at the Oscars every year.

These girls are such fine actresses that, disappointingly, viewers rarely get to see their true feelings. But on the following occasion, the young lady in question was adhering to the much more entertaining philosophy of 'It's not the winning that matters – it's the being taken apart that counts'.

In one of the earliest examples of bad loserdom, the public encountered the fabulous Marina Papaelia, who taught us how to squawk like an Egyptian way back in 1953, when the Miss World contest was barely two years old.

If Marina was competing in pageants today, footage of her Miss World appearance would almost certainly become a rapid YouTube favourite.

In his 1967 book, *The Miss World Story*, Eric Morley proclaimed Marina Papaelia as "the greatest showman of them all", and even 60 years later there have been few contestants to challenge that title.

In language that in today's politically correct age would make Miss World President Julia Morley faint with horror, Eric, in his autobiography, recollects Marina as being "very attractive, but slightly overweight, as Egyptian girls are inclined to be at her age".

She was a colourful character from the moment she arrived in London for the contest. The 22 year old Greek-Egyptian brunette was apparently able to shout insults in five languages, resulting in her room-mate, Miss Denmark, demanding to change rooms after just one night in her company. Nobody else would subsequently share with Marina, so she had the room to herself.

Such was her overwhelming personality, Eric recalled, that she had to constantly be the centre of attention, and her sense of unshakeable self-belief meant that she was convinced that she only had to turn up to win the crown.

Yet she quickly established herself as the other contestants' shop steward. They would take their complaints to her, and she would represent them in front of the boss.

One of the events leading up to the contest was a night out in London at the expense of the sponsors. The girls were all briefed beforehand to be, as Eric Morley put it, on their best behaviour.

To Marina, this was her chance to shine. The club in Bond Street was packed with guests eager to mingle with the Miss World contestants, and she intended to take full advantage.

As soon as the orchestra struck up, she kicked off her shoes and leapt onto the dance floor with her bemused partner, singing along loudly as she twirled around. Eric recalled how she caused such a stir that the other guests stood back to watch, and then gave her a huge round of applause at the end of the number.

Eric says he ordered the dancing queen to sit down and to stop drawing attention to herself, but his words were in vain. The next thing he knew, the club had practically emptied, with the manager apoplectic at the thought of all that lost revenue.

They soon discovered what had caused the mass exodus. Marina had taken herself to the foyer, perched herself on the counter, and was in the middle of performing a one-woman chat show for her enraptured audience.

Miss Egypt's impromptu turn made headline news the next day, and the press quickly installed her as their favourite to win the contest. Eric Morley himself developed a soft spot for her, despite her unwillingness to play ball. "You couldn't really lose your temper with her," he wrote, "because she had such a good sense of humour".

However, his patience was to be sorely tested further on the night of the final. Mecca had just signed a contract with the BBC to start filming the contest for newsreels worldwide. Although the Corporation wouldn't start screening the Miss World contest live until 1959, this early deal was a massive coup for Mecca and Eric was determined that nothing would threaten it.

When Morley realised the show was running over schedule and the audience were starting a slow clapping of hands to express their frustration, he fled backstage to try and discover the reason. Once there, he found Marina sobbing hysterically in the dressing room, refusing to change into her swimsuit. "I don't want to go back on stage," he recalled her yelling in her heavy accent. "I don't want to have anything more to do with this".

The chaperone explained that when Marina had paraded in her evening gown, she'd been incensed to hear that Miss France had received a more enthusiastic response from the audience than her. Her implication was that if Marina wasn't the absolute favourite with the audience, she didn't want to carry on.

Mindful of his fledgling and lucrative contract with the BBC, in despair Eric decided to appeal to Marina's vanity to persuade her into her swimsuit. "With your figure, the judges are bound to take a good look", he said to her.

It worked, and when Marina made the final five she believed that now nothing could stand in her way of the crown. What she didn't yet know was that among the judges – who included actors David Niven and Margaret Lockwood - there was a split vote between herself, Miss France and Miss Switzerland, and that the final casting vote put her into an unacceptable third place.

When her name was announced, she walked out with a look of pure disdain on her face and, in front of the audience and the TV cameras, collapsed to the floor in a crumpled, dramatic heap.

The *Daily Mirror* the next morning was headlined, "The Victor and The Vanquished", contrasting a photo of the new Miss World, France's Denise Perrier, with one of the hysterical Miss Egypt lying prostrate at the new queen's feet.

Marina made a miraculous recovery to be interviewed by reporters after the contest and, in a comment that has gone down in the Miss World annals of history, when asked how she felt about Miss France, replied: "I theenk she steenk".

Said winner Denise Perrier, when interviewed in 1976 for Don Short's book *Miss World The Naked Truth*: "Of course it was very embarrassing at the time, but I have long since forgiven her. Marina just didn't think she could possibly lose".

Lose she did, but she remains to this day a treasured memory in the Miss World hall of infamy.

"Despite the headaches and frights she gave me at the time, I shall always remember her as one of the outstanding figures, in every way, among all those who have entered the contest at any time," wrote Eric in his 1967 book.

As a final tribute to the Egyptian spitfire, the following year, when Miss Egypt, Antigone Costanda, won the 1954 Miss World contest, the new queen announced to the press afterwards that it was a victory not just for her, but for Marina as well.

Lesley Langley

"God, I was gorgeous!"

Lesley Langley, Miss World 1965

In his 1967 book, *The Miss World Story*, Eric Morley said: "There have been three British winners [until that point] and all of them in varying ways have caused me to lose sleep."

Lesley Langley gave Eric no less than three periods of prolonged insomnia during her year of office.

A tall, blonde model from Weymouth, Lesley won the Miss United Kingdom contest in 1965, and was represented in her career by a well-known London agent called Pat Larthe.

Despite rules that state that all third party representation must be declared before the Miss World contest, Lesley decided not to confess her situation to Eric until just days before the final.

Worse, she had signed a document – as had all the contestants – declaring that she was free of any agency or management agreements.

The Morleys have never made any bones about insisting that they are the winner's sole agent for the duration of her reign. Not only does it simplify the process for interested advertisers and sponsors, but it also ensures maximum profit for Mecca, the then Miss World organisers – and indeed, the winner herself.

Eric says in his book, "I wasn't too worried when I heard that Lesley had an agent because I didn't think she would win Miss World". In fact, Eric favoured Miss USA that year, who eventually finished second.

Lesley confirmed in a 1998 BBC documentary, *In Reverse Order*, that Eric believed her chances were slim. "He called me into his office before the contest and told me he didn't think I would win, that I wasn't right for it."

However, win Lesley did – and the result opened up a second can of worms.

She was the second successive Miss UK to win the title, and the third in five years. The press immediately caught on to the obvious implication of so many Brits succeeding in a British show, hosted in Britain.

Like Eric Morley, Miss USA's promoter, Alfred Patricelli, fully expected his contestant, Dianne Lyn Batts, to win. When she finished second to Lesley, he told the press, "This looks really bad, with three British girls having won in five years. The chances against this happening are enormous."

Others also queried Lesley's status of having an agent. Should she not be disqualified for this, they asked. And was the contest fixed for so many British girls to win?

Eric Morley was forced to reveal the final scores. Five of the nine judges – which included American singer Johnny Mathis, French actress Martine Carol, and The Marchioness of Tavistock – gave Lesley their first place.

Bombarded by reporters and their incessant demands for answers, Eric admitted he nearly made the decision to pack it in. "For a while I felt like putting an end to the contest for good," he said. "It didn't seem worth all the bother".

When he met up with Lesley the day after the crowning, though, he assured her that she wouldn't be fired for bending the rules.

It was then that she dropped another bombshell: not only did she have an agent, she also employed a manager. Added to which, they both wanted full control of her year of office.

This would mean that Eric and Mecca would be unable to make any bookings on her behalf, and would have to direct all queries to her management. In other words, Eric wouldn't make a penny out of her reign.

Lesley asked Eric if Mecca could represent her as well, but he curtly refused, unwilling to share his carefully-honed contacts with the other parties.

The ensuring row was leaked to the press, and they portrayed Lesley as the victim of Mecca's heartless refusal to promote or support her as a result of the situation.

With Lesley's reign off to the worst possible start, Eric had one more reason to reach for the sleeping pills.

For the first time in the history of the Miss World contest, nude photographs of the winner were published in a British magazine, before being syndicated worldwide.

The contest sponsors – especially those from Catholic countries - were furious. They accused Lesley of ruining the reputation of Miss World and threatened to withdraw their services altogether.

Eric managed to avoid a full-scale revolt by assuring the sponsors that the photos of Lesley were taken many months before the contest and that even she herself didn't know that they would ever re-surface.

With great naivety and irony in retrospect, Eric said at the time, "I can only hope that we shall not have a similar problem again".

Little did he know that Lesley's candid shots were only the first in a very long line of nude and topless pictures that would, quite literally, expose many a Miss World contestant and winner right up to the present day.

Lesley and Eric managed to get through the rest of the year without further hazard, but the blonde beauty had a final parting shot to end her tumultuous year.

She refused to attend the 1966 final, citing a previous engagement. This decision was not entirely without reason. Eric had made plans to invite a celebrity to crown the new winner instead, and had only backtracked and asked Lesley in the light of accusations of spite towards her.

Talking to *The Observer* in 2001, Lesley looked back at the problems she had faced nearly 35 years previously:

"Eric Morley and I did not get on at all. He didn't like the fact that I already had an agent. Mecca wanted to represent you because they took something like 25 per cent of the fee, whereas my agent was taking 10. Morley didn't want me to win - and he was on the panel of judges, it was very unfair - but they outvoted him.

"There were three Miss UKs in five years, but there's no way it was fixed, because if anything he would have tried to fix it for me not to win. After me, they made the girls sign a contract upfront, saying that they would be represented by Mecca solely."

One good thing came out of Lesley's reign – she met her future husband, jazz musician Alan Haven and they later had a daughter. Now divorced and living back in her hometown of Weymouth with current partner Richard Porter, Lesley last worked as a receptionist at a private dental practice.

She remembers that in those days "there just weren't as many options. And maybe we relied on our looks more. But now there are the supermodels - there have always been glamorous women cashing in on their looks. I suppose if you've got it, you've got to use it a bit in this world today - and people do, everybody does."

When she looks back through all the old photographs now, she says, she can truly appreciate the looks she had.

"God, I was gorgeous!"

Miss World 1970

"Ban this disgraceful cattle market!"

Women's Liberation protesters at Miss World 1970

Bob Hope's Miss World career will be remembered primarily for two reasons: his alleged long-standing affair with 1961 winner Rosemarie Frankland and for the feminists and flour bombs spectacle of 1970.

The first Miss World contest of the decade was an early indication of a turning of the tide. Almost overnight, the show had gone from a hugely popular TV show to, in some quarters, a cattle market of distasteful and demeaning proportions.

The world was changing, and the 1970 contest reflected the groundswell of opinion that was making itself heard both morally and politically. Apartheid and feminism was suddenly knocking on the door of Miss World Ltd.

The first public show of anti-pageant feminism had occurred with a bra-burning ceremony at the Miss America contest in 1968, and soon the movement had reached London.

Women were slowly being woken to the notion of equality in the workplace and to challenging the concept of the nuclear family in which they were relegated to the kitchen.

The Miss World contest, where women were judged purely on their looks, was a natural target.

The 1970 contest had started off on a wrong footing. For the first time, two women from South Africa were taking part – one black (Miss Africa South), and one white (Miss South Africa).

This move was construed by many as acceptance of apartheid and one of the protesters in 1970 was a certain Peter Hain, a future Cabinet Minister in the 1997 Labour government. Hain was spokesman for the militant youth wing of the Liberal Party and promised to demonstrate against the inclusion of one black and one white contestant because it would "propagate the policy of apartheid", adding that the move was, "an incredibly arrogant insult to Britain's black community".

At the same time, a televised debate saw Eric Morley pitted against Helen Tovey of the Young Liberals. In response to her accusation of the contest being a 'cattle market', Morley replied, "Now here we have a young lady who is a frustrated runner-up in a beauty contest. Frustrated women who don't win always want to kick up a row about something."

It was still among the most viewed TV shows – over 23m tuned in that year, the most-watched programme of 1970 – but a rebel faction was moving in and by all accounts it was here to stay as long as Miss World dared to be around.

In the early hours of the morning before the contest, a small bomb exploded under a BBC outside broadcasting van, planted by an extremist group, the Angry Brigade, to try and stop the show. Nobody was injured, but the 5,000 guests filing into the Royal Albert Hall for the final were subjected to demonstrators protesting from behind police barricades, chanting their slogan, "We're not beautiful, we're not ugly, we're angry!" Security was on high alert.

Michael Aspel was the main host of the show, with Bob Hope as a special guest invited to perform the crowning of the winner. When introduced towards the end of the contest, his sexist comments served only to fan the flames of the objectors.

"It's been quite a cattle market," he announced. "I've been backstage checking calves." His jokes fell on stony ears to a largely unresponsive audience.

One section of the audience was preparing for action. Their cue was a football rattle reverberating around the silent hall. At this sudden interruption, Hope broke off from his sentence and looked up, seemingly dumbfounded.

At that moment, a flour bomb exploded behind him, and the auditorium erupted into a cacophony of whistles and shouting. A group of about fifty women, and a handful of men, stood up with placards, shouting "Women's liberation!", and "We are liberationists, ban this disgraceful cattle market!"

Ink bombs, stink bombs, tomatoes and leaflets were thrown onto the stage along with the flour. A rattle was thrown at the judges, who included actresses Joan Collins and Susannah York, and singer Glen Campbell. The Albert Hall filled with the stench of smoke and contest officials struggled to eject the protesters and restore order.

Bob Hope had long since fled off stage into the wings.

Years later, Eric Morley revealed in a TV documentary that Hope had been prevented from scarpering completely by his wife Julia. "She had hold of his ankle so that he couldn't run away," he laughed. "When I invited him back on stage and introduced him as 'a very brave man', Julia said to me afterwards – 'Brave man, my foot! I've been holding onto the so-and-so to keep him there!'".

Michael Aspel remembers Hope's reaction when he went back onstage. "We all thought, now he'll sort them out, he'll give them what for. But he seemed incredibly rattled, and came out with an extraordinary monologue about how, if people could break up an affair as beautiful as this, they've got to be on some sort of dope".

Hope was also alleged to have then turned away from the microphone and said, "Who are these bastards?"

The eventual winner, Grenada's Jennifer Hosten, said that when she spoke to Bob Hope months later, during their visit to Vietnam, he told her that he had been "very shaken and very angry at the breach of security that night which had put him in such a position and that he wouldn't ever consider appearing at such an event again."

Sally Alexander was one of the protesters that night. "Our targets were the people who ran Miss World," she said in an interview with *The Observer*, "The object of our anger and our frustration was, as we saw it, a system that left women with no other economic opportunities, except cleaning, or low-paid jobs at the very bottom of the wage hierarchy. So we decided to make a spectacle out of the event."

Fellow protester Jo Robinson explained that the demonstration wasn't against the contestants. "We didn't want to be seen to be attacking them in any way, but the idea of a beauty contest was an obvious target for feminists as it represented how women at that time were being objectified as sexual stereotypes".

Sally Alexander remembers her surprise at the support her group received from the girls themselves. "As we were arrested and dragged out, we bumped into the contestants, most of whom were very nice to us, and said, 'Let them alone, they're only having their say' - that kind of stuff."

Julia Morley wished the demonstrators had sought her out at the time. "I had a lot of sympathy for women's lib," she said in the same *Observer* interview. "The only thing that I found very difficult was that they didn't actually come to see me or talk to me.

DAILY Mirror

MISS WORLD!

WHAT a beauty! She is the new Miss World... 22-year-old Jennifer Hosten of Grenada, the smallest country to have a competitor. And she was letting none of the nonsense that followed her victory upset her last night. "I'm absolutely delighted," she said.

Miss Grenada snatched the golden title in an exciting finish from fifty-seven other contestants.

Now fame and fortune await the dark-skinned beauty in her year of reign as Miss World.

The first prize alone wins her £2,500.

As she awakes this morning, to a champagne breakfast and showers of good wishes, the new Miss World can also look forward to an income of £50,000 from modelling fees.

6d. Saturday, November 21, 1970 No. 20,805

IN THE MIRROR ON MONDAY

The truth about Marianne

An exclusive, revealing and astonishing interview with Marianne Faithfull, golden girl of the pop scene by...
DONALD ZEC

THE BRIGHTER SIDE OF MONDAY

It's the darkest day of the week, Monday. There's no one better to brighten it up than

KEITH WATERHOUSE

IN THE MIRROR ON MONDAY

The new Miss World.. Jennifer Hosten

AND OH, WHAT A WILD WORLD!

Story by KENELM JENOUR: Picture by ARTHUR SIDEY

BEAUTIFUL Jennifer Hosten, 22-year-old Miss Grenada, was crowned last night as the new Miss World ... and, oh, what a wild, wild world it was.

Smoke bombs, stink bombs and a shower of leaflets were hurled on to the stage as comedian Bob Hope wisecracked to the audience before the final parade.

A home-made bomb exploded under a BBC television van outside the Royal Albert Hall before the show.

Bewildered

Gangs of demonstrators holding banners saying: "You Poor Cows," mobbed the fifty-eight lovely contestants as they arrived in coaches.

There were protests galore after the show when it was revealed that one of the judges was the Prime Minister of Grenada.

No wonder the new Miss World's first public words were: "I'm bewildered."

So were thousands of the 30,000,000 viewers who watched the parade of beauty on BBC.

They rang the BBC, the organisers know, and the Daily Mirror, in angry complaint.

One amazed viewer said: "I will never know how the judges chose her — the smallest haven't been in the last fifteen."

Another wondered: "How on earth was the Prime Minister of Grenada allowed to be a judge?"

No one answered that.

Whistles

And the new Miss World was most diplomatic. She said: "I think the girls who enter should be proud that they can represent their countries here in Britain."

But what a night it was !

Bob Hope was halfway through his patter to the audience when chaos erupted.

Whistles were blown and a football rattle suddenly sounded at the rear of the auditorium.

Then a number of demonstrators rushed towards the stage.

Stink bombs, smoke bombs and leaflets showered around him. Mr. Hope retreated as stewards dashed in and hurried the

■ Continued on Back Page

At the time, I was actually very much involved, and trying really hard to change things, but it takes time."

The contest reached its conclusion without further disruption, but more controversy was only around the corner. Rank outside Jennifer

Hosten, Miss Grenada, was crowned the winner, and the resulting protest almost equalled that of the earlier kerfuffle.

With Miss Grenada the winner, and Miss Africa South taking the runner-up position, it was the first time that two black women had taken the top spots in a major beauty contest.

Angry callers jammed the switchboards of the newspapers on Fleet Street and the BBC was deluged with protests about the judges' choice. Their main – and not unreasonable – gripe centred on the fact that one of the judges was the Prime Minister of Grenada, Sir Eric Gairy.

A group gathered outside the Albert Hall chanting, "Swe-den! Sweden!" in defiance of the fact that the hot favourite had finished only fourth. It transpired that four of the judges had put Sweden first, while only two had given Grenada top marks.

The days ahead saw the row only deepen over allegations of "rigging", so much so that Julia resigned her post as organising director. "I am deeply ashamed at the allegations this man has had to face", she stormed, in support of the Grenadian Prime Minister. "Perhaps I was just not the right person to organise the contest. I have had enough".

Meanwhile in Grenada, opposition leader Herbert Blaize slammed Mr Gairy's decision to join the judging panel, amidst rumours of a business deal between the Premier and the Morleys, involving the opening of a Mecca casino on the island. This accusation was denied by both Eric Morley and a director of Grand Metropolitan Hotels, an organisation with which Mecca had recently merged.

In an attempt to diffuse the row, Eric Morley put the judges' scorecards on view. He had adopted the Majority Vote System for the judging procedure in the '50s, which he had hoped would eliminate any possibility of collusion or favoritism. But it also came across as a terribly complex and complicated system to explain to an outsider.

However, this move appeased the baying protesters and reputations were restored, with Julia Morley returning to office. Many still felt that the presence of Sir Gairy on the judging panel had influenced the other judges to give Jennifer token placings, and Miss Sweden was said, years later, to still feel cheated out of the title.

Jennifer Hosten calmly sidestepped the controversy and became a national heroine on the Spice Island of Grenada. Six commemorative stamps were issued in her honour, and in 1978 she was appointed High Commissioner to Canada from Grenada.

In 2005 she returned to the Miss World stage as one of several former winners invited to judge the contest. That year, nobody quibbled about the results. She now organises the Miss Grenada contests, the winners going forward to the Miss World final.

As for the South Africa controversy, the two-girl policy lasted for six years. In 1976, nine governments ordered their contestants to withdraw from Miss World in protest, and the Miss Africa South contest was scrapped as a result. However, ten governments still objected to the presence of a white Miss South Africa the following year, causing another mass walk-out. South African contestants were banned from competing at Miss World thereafter from 1978 until 1991.

The Miss Universe pageant was largely unaffected by apartheid demonstrations, but it is highly symbolic to note that in 1977 Janelle Commissiong, from Trinidad & Tobago, became the first black woman to win Miss Universe, and that one year later she was crowning her successor....white South African Margaret Gardiner.

Jacqui Mofokeng became the first black woman to win the Miss South Africa title in 1993, causing Nelson Mandela to proclaim that, "any victory for one black South African is a victory for us all".

In an interesting footnote, Eric Gairy was overthrown as Prime Minister of Grenada in 1979 due to allegations of corruption, favouritism and abuse of human rights.

The Miss World 1970 saga was mentioned on BBC radio once again in 2011, when the contest's controversial result using the Majority Vote System was compared to the 'unjust' result which would occur in a UK general election if the same system – known in this case as the Alternative Vote – were adopted in a national poll instead of the current First Past The Post.

In the subsequent referendum, Miss Sweden would no doubt have been delighted to learn that the public overwhelming voted to reject the AV system as overly complex and ultimately unfair.

Joyce McKinney

"I would ski nude down Mount Everest..."

Joyce McKinney, Miss Wyoming 1972

J oyce McKinney wasn't a reigning beauty queen at the time of her controversy, nor was it connected in any way with her appearance on the catwalk.

Nevertheless, no book about scandalous lovelies would be complete without documenting the astonishing story of the *'Sex in Chains'* case that dominated tabloid headlines for months.

It was the ultimate tabloid scoop – beauty, kinky sex, religion, kidnap. Little wonder it turfed Jim Callaghan and Johnny Rotten off the newspaper front pages back in 1977.

Joyce's story begins when, as a university student in East Tennessee, she joined the Church of the Latter Day Saints, having been convinced that this was the route to finding the man of her dreams.

Joyce's natural sense of the dramatic led to her entering beauty pageants. She won the Miss Wyoming title in 1972, despite having never visited the state previously, and took part in that year's Miss USA final.

Defeated yet unbowed, she signed up to study drama at Utah University – and that's when the man of her dreams really did appear.

Failing to win the affections of fellow Mormon, pop star Wayne Osmond, Joyce began a relationship with another devotee, Kirk

Anderson. She insisted they fell in love on their first date and were soon planning a wedding but, under pressure from his family and the bishop, he ended the brief relationship, moving from Utah to California. Joyce, unable to accept his decision, followed, and pursued him so relentlessly that he requested an overseas posting to England in the summer of 1976.

Joyce was determined to trace him. She hired a private detective, who tracked him down to where he had made his new home in Surrey. Along with a friend, Keith May - who himself was allegedly obsessed with Joyce – she flew to the UK and they found Kirk Anderson at the Church of the Latter Day Saints in Ewell.

The pair, armed with imitation guns and a bottle of chloroform, bundled Kirk into a car and took him to a rented cottage in Devon, where they held him hostage for three days.

During the court case that followed, Kirk told how Joyce made it clear to him that he would not be freed until he agreed to marry her. He was tied in spreadeagled position to the bed, his arms and legs shackled with leather straps, padlocks, chains and ropes. Joyce tore the pyjamas from his body and forced him to have intercourse with her against his will.

Joyce insisted on her moment in the witness box at a bail hearing and proved herself to be fabulously uninhibited. Kirk, she insisted, found sexual bondage a turn on "because then he doesn't have to feel guilty". Moreover, because his mother was "over-dominant", he was excited at the thought of being powerless before a woman, and she gave him oral sex only upon his request. He had to have the lights off during sex, she continued, and always had to wash afterwards.

It was all consensual, she insisted, pointing out the unlikelihood of "a little 8-stone girl like me" overcoming a tall, 18 stone man, with thighs as wide as her waist.

BIGGER, BETTER VALUE

DAILY EXPRESS

THE VOICE OF BRITAIN

No. 24,225 Monday May 22 1978 Weather: Sunny spells 8p ★★★

McKINNEY'S OWN STORY

In the paper that found her—the scoop they tried to ban

MY UNDYING LOVE

I still want my Mormon, Joyce tells the Express

By Peter Tory and Brian Vine in Atlanta, Georgia

FOR the first time yesterday Joyce McKinney talked freely about the love affair behind her astonishing sex-in-chains kidnapping case.

She was taking a breather in her escape trail across America to talk only to the Express — the paper that found her in Georgia last week.

Her love for Mormon priest Kirk Anderson whom she was accused of kidnapping is, she says, " tender, profound and indestructible."

"I had waited 24 years for a man like Kirk to come along to

give myself to and he was perfect," she said.

"I'll always love him and will probably never marry anyone else. If he comes to me she says he's sorry for all the lies he told to court I will forgive him and devote the rest of my life to him.

"Our love affair was not squalid, perverted and untidy, as the police and the Mormons would have the British people believe."

Joyce, 29, was speaking on a holiday beach, somewhere on the coast of America—a girl on the run from British law and in fear of arrest by American police along with friend and co-defendant Keith May.

LOVE NEST

She revealed that during the three days and nights in her remote Devon "love nest" with Kirk—a weekend which led to her being sent for trial on the kidnapping charge—he was a willing partner of his bondage, tied to a bed while they made love.

"Anyway I tired upset and clumsy to tie him to the bed—so I'm really the tie-up-ropes girl not the sex-in-chains lady," she drawled in her Southern accent.

"The whole thing about this bondage is the transference of guilt. His being tied up at his request transfers the blame for sex to the partner. Mormon priests are taught to believe that sex is not for pleasure."

She told how, three years ago, she first made love to Kirk when they

The REAL Joyce McKinney yesterday...sporting a carnation, symbol of the sex-in-chains case. MORE William Lovelace pictures inside

THE REAL McKINNEY: SEE PAGE 19

Page 3, Column 4.

In a quote that has gone down in the fables of history Joyce added, in her Southern Belle drawl, "I loved Kirk so much I would have skied down Mount Everest in the nude with a carnation up my nose".

She'd met Kirk, she said, in 1975 and thought she had found true love with a boy she could read the Bible with. She had spent her life savings following him across the world but, she sobbed in court, he had no idea what eternal love was and she wanted nothing more to do with him. He had lied in court, she said, due to his fear of being ex-communicated by the Church.

Just before the trial in May 1978, when Joyce and her accomplice Keith May were about to face charges of kidnapping (a rape charge could not at that time be brought if the victim was a man) they failed to report on bail to West Hendon police station. Using false passports and disguising themselves as members of a deaf and dumb acting troupe, they relied on the pity of airport staff at London Heathrow to wave them through the normal security checks, and boarded a flight to Ireland.

From Shannon airport, they then caught an Air Canada flight to Toronto, whereupon a stewardess recognised the couple from newspaper photographs.

This gave the tabloids – already hugely excited about the case – carte blanche to print all the salacious details they had been hitherto forced to withhold about the North Carolina blonde's soft porn career and her numerous skeletons.

Magazines and newspapers fell over themselves to be the first to track her down to where she and Keith May had holed up in the States. The *Daily Mirror* even published a special booklet in tribute to the case, while *The Sun* produced a mocked-up cartoon of Joyce skiing nude down a mountain with a carnation up her nose. This was tabloid sensationalism at its very best.

Later, Joyce was sentenced, in her absence, to one year in prison – a sentence she has yet to serve. She re-surfaced in 1984 when she audaciously began stalking Kirk Anderson – who by this time was married with three children - yet again, outside his workplace in Salt Lake City. Long-suffering Kirk made a citizen's arrest and complained, justifiably, that his life was being torn apart for a second time. Joyce's lawyer argued that his client had wanted to see him purely "for old time's sake" and to make sure that he was happy.

In 2008, the owner of the first litter of commercially cloned dogs, calling herself Bernann McKinney, made the headlines due to the scientific breakthrough of the experiment. It wasn't long before some of the older British tabloid reporters recognised her as Joyce, the subject of so many of their headlines of thirty years before.

And Joyce became the subject of fascination for a whole new generation upon the 2011 release of *Tabloid*, a documentary film that told the whole extraordinary story for cinema audiences.

The *Daily Mail* tracked her down as a result of this fresh wave of publicity to her home in North Carolina where they found a 60 year old, overweight figure, a million miles from the blonde bombshell of old – yet seemingly just as deluded.

She told the reporter, "I'm elderly now, I have a heart condition, I'm crippled and partially blind. I'm just a little old lady, looking back, eyes misting, on an incredible lost love."

There had been, she said, no romance in her life since the manacled Mormon. "I was afraid to have a love affair of any kind after Kirk, I was afraid to kiss a man. So I chose just to be celibate. As Bridget Bardot once said: 'I gave my youth to men and I give my old age to dogs.' Dogs and children love Joyce McKinney, they sense in me an innocence, a gentleness".

No, she wouldn't be going to see the film, she said. "He loved me. This wasn't a story of requited love."

Neighbours in her childhood town of Minneapolis saw Joyce as a very different character to the lovable eccentric portrayed in the film. They remember her as litigious to the point of paranoia – even suing a neighbour due to its barking dog – as well as having psychiatric treatment for drug abuse and several run-ins with the law for theft and threatening behaviour, among others.

Kirk Anderson is now an estate agent, living a quiet life with his family, while co-conspirator Keith May died in 2004.

But there is no question that Joyce's name – and her story – will live on forever. The producer of *Tabloid* could, he said, even see a musical or opera based on her exploits. "She sees herself as this princess who crosses the ocean with her conspirators to save her prince."

With, we must assume, a carnation up her nose.

Susan Cuff

"It's all so silly - I've never met the judges"

Susan Cuff, Miss Great Britain 1975

In scenes that brought back echoes of the crowning ceremony of Miss World 1953, Susan Cuff's triumph as Miss Great Britain in 1975 was marred by those who had fallen by the judges' wayside.

As she was announced the winner, twelve of the twenty contestants stormed off stage in disgust at the decision. Although the contest wasn't being screened live, the cameras were recording the event for broadcast at a later date, and the girls refused to return to the stage to allow re-filming of the final segment.

So what had poor Susan done to deserve such a boycott?

Let's rewind a few months, to where Susan was named runner-up in Mecca's Miss United Kingdom contest in Blackpool. As was then traditional, the girl who was placed second in Miss UK – in this case, Susan – was given the title of Miss Britain and entry into the big Miss International pageant in Tokyo.

However, earlier in the year Susan had also qualified for the final of the Miss Great Britain contest. This show was run by Lancaster Corporation and Mecca saw the contest as their deadly rival. As a result, any girl who chose to enter Miss Great Britain was barred by Mecca from also entering their Miss United Kingdom contests.

Presented with the choice between carrying on as Mecca's Miss Britain, or joining the rival Miss Great Britain final, Susan chose the latter. As a result of her decision, Mecca stripped her of her Miss Britain title, in a move that courted plenty of press attention.

This publicity was the reason for her Miss Great Britain rivals' upset when she beat them to the crown. They saw it as an unfair advantage that, they believed, had resulted in swaying the judges' decision.

One riled contestant said afterwards, "I've never seen girls so upset in a beauty contest. It's not a question of being catty. We asked to see the voting slips but were refused".

Another declared that the judges were "biased towards Susan before the contest even started".

Susan was understandably upset by the fracas. "I just took a gamble," she said. "It's all so silly – I've never met the judges".

One of those judges that night was the late, lamented columnist Lynda Lee-Potter. In her next column for the *Daily Mail*, she wrote of her experiences.

"I've never actually believed all those hoary old tales about beauty queens hating each other's 36-23-36, with their aggressive ambitious mums screaming at the end, 'Our Doreen should've won, disqualify the judges', but I know now they're TRUE.

"I honestly couldn't have tried to be fairer. I couldn't have given a damn who won as long as she was the prettiest. I had never clapped eyes on nor read one word about the winner before she became Miss GB, and I was just a teeny little bit upset to find myself in the middle of a humdinger of a row and noisily accused of being part of a rigged contest.

"About two-thirds of those girls, gifted only with good looks, gave a bad-tempered display of petty spite and showed enough narcissistic temperament to make Billy Bremner look like a beginner."

The runner-up in the contest, Christine Owen (later to become a hostess of TV's *Sale of the Century*) agreed. "They thought Susan had stayed in the contest because she had inside information that she was a sure favourite," she said.

"That's nonsense – she's a lovely girl and deserved to win. The girls who kicked up a stink and walked off want their bottoms spanked".

After a rather muted celebration dinner following the contest, officials of Lancaster Corporation finally agreed to unlock the safe and show the girls the judges' voting slips. These proved that there had been no mistake – Susan was the clear winner, with 184 points out of 200.

Susan went on to become hostess of the long-running quiz show *Mr & Mrs* – with her catchphrase, 'Take care, lots of care' - before marrying then sports journalist, David Davies, who later become Chief Executive of the Football Association.

They remain happily married today with two daughters, one of whom, Amanda, is a sports presenter for CNN International.

This isn't the only occasion of a girl being forced to choose between the rival factions and then winning. Michelle Hobson was told to either forego her place in Miss Great Britain 1980, or in Morley's Miss England.

Michelle, like Susan, plumped for Miss GB. And like Susan, she won. On that occasion however, the also-rans remained firmly on the stage behind her, smiling and clapping gamely.

Sian Adey-Jones

"I kicked him as hard as I could"

Sian Adey-Jones, Miss Wales 1976

They called her 'the Welsh wildcat'. Two years after being rocked by the Helen Morgan scandal, the valleys found themselves adorned with yet another wayward beauty queen, but this time for very different reasons.

Sian Adey-Jones was the stunning blonde who took the Miss Wales crown in 1976 and finished third in the Miss Universe pageant. She won the runner-up spot in the Miss United Kingdom contest and prepared to settle down and enjoy the rest of her reign as Miss Wales.

But it was life away from the catwalk that generated more headlines than all her beauty queen triumphs put together.

Sian's first calamity happened while she was being driven to open a factory in South Wales, as one of her official duties during her year's reign as Miss Wales.

The 73 year old driver of the estate car blacked out en route. The car careered round a bend and smashed into an oncoming van.

Sian was trapped on the floor of the vehicle, blinded by blood and cut by flying glass.

In a 1984 interview with the *News of the World*, she recalled the horror of that day:

"Normally I hated travelling in the back seat because I get car sick. It was a strange thing, but instinctively that day I forced myself to get into the back.

"It was a four-hour trip and I started to doze off, but I didn't like the way he was driving. The car was careering all over the place.

"The next moment I felt the car losing it on a bend. There was a thud. I was waiting for the bang but I didn't expect such a terrific explosion. I was flung forward and trapped on the floor behind the passenger seat. Then I heard this drip drip drip.

"I thought, 'Jesus, the car's going to go up in flames and I'm trapped inside.' I lifted my head and realised that it was my face that was dripping. Blood was streaming from my eyes and blinding me.

"Later, I learned that the bonnet of the car had curled backwards and embedded itself in the front passenger seat. If I'd been sitting there I'd have had my head off".

Sian was rushed to Wrexham Hospital, where she faced more horror. "I remember hearing this nurse say 'Ugh!' when she saw me".

For a young woman whose face was her fortune, the reactions of the nursing staff and her family confirmed her greatest fears.

Said Sian, "I later learned that the hospital had telephoned my Mum to warn her of the state of my face. My younger sister arrived first and collapsed, weeping uncontrollably. But nobody would give me a mirror, saying they were too busy".

She was transferred to hospital in Liverpool for a four-and-a-half hour operation on her face, involving two surgeons painstakingly affecting repairs with one hundred stitches.

"I was bandaged up like a Mummy," she recalled, but seized her chance after the operation to investigate. "I staggered to the toilet and took the bandages off. I saw it staring back at me from the mirror. Something that I didn't recognise at all.

There wasn't even a trace of what I looked like. It was red, raw and swollen with a black spider web of tiny stitches everywhere.

"It was like the end of me – I just wept and wept".

Back home in Clwyd, her small nephew recoiled in disgust at his first sight of her, and when she braved the local pub, "everybody was nearly in tears, shuffling in their seats and looking away".

Sian moved into her boyfriend Steve Cryer's house in Llandudno and retreated into her shell. At her six-monthly check-up her surgeon reiterated that no more could be done for her. She turned down invitations to functions and found it impossible to accept that her modelling and beauty queen careers were over.

It was a rare night out, then, in November 1976, which led to Sian's most infamous episode. Steve had persuaded his depressed girlfriend to accompany him to a dinner party with mutual friends.

On the way home, as they drove through Colwyn Bay, the couple were stopped by a policeman and policewoman on suspicion of drunk-driving.

Steve was asked to take a breath test and Sian took the opportunity of spraying a mint breath spray into his mouth. WPC Patricia Evans reached into Sian's bag to grab the spray, and Sian bent her fingers back in an attempt to remove her hands.

The *Daily Express* reported that Sian then got out of the car and kicked the policeman between his legs while "screaming and swearing hysterically".

In court, the policeman involved, PC Colin Avery, told how her kick was "very painful. Once I'd regained my composure I slapped her across the face in an effort to calm her, but it had no effect whatsoever."

DAILY Mirror

BRITAIN'S BIGGEST DAILY SALE   7p   Tuesday, May 10, 1977

'WILDCAT' MISS WALES .. and a blow below the belt

BEAUTY QUEEN - Sian

ACCUSED: Sian Adey-Jones yesterday. She pleads not guilty to assault.

GET SET FOR PRICE WAR

By DAVID RADCLIFFE

BEAUTY queen Sian Adey-Jones fought like a "wildcat" with police, a court heard yesterday.

Sian 'kicked and spat in breath-test battle'

Kicked

Policeman Avery.

When arrested and taken to the police van, she spat twice in his face and shouted, "F*** off, you pig". At the police station, as PC Avery led to her to a cell she turned round, back-heeled him and kicked him very hard once in the testicles. As he fell to his knees, Sian said, "Good. I will ruin you."

Once in the cell she became violent again and it took three police officers to restrain her and hold her down as two removed her cowboy boots and jewellery, during which time she was struggling and yelled, "I am a wildcat!"

During the court case, the prosecutor called it "a disgraceful episode. She was shouting at the top of her voice, her language was appalling and she was unsteady on her feet."

Sian denied the assault vehemently and such was the conflicting evidence presented in court that she was found guilty of assaulting the policewoman, but cleared of attacking PC Avery. The prosecutor admitted afterwards that "someone was lying through their teeth. Beautiful people lie as well, and lie beautifully."

She was fined £100 and ordered to pay costs of £250, and £25 compensation to the policewoman. A cross summons her lawyers had issued against PC Avery for his slapping of her face was dropped.

The story was a sensation and made headlines all over the world, with the media readily adopting the "Welsh Wildcat" nickname.

Sian recalled the episode many years later. "The whole thing got out of hand," she admitted.

"We started giggling when the police couldn't find their breathalyser. I took a breath freshener out of my bag and the policeman demanded to see it.

"I got angry, then the policewoman dragged me out of the car and the policeman grabbed me.

"I told him he was hurting but he wouldn't listen. He bent my wrists so I kicked him as hard as I could.

"He went down on his knees, came back up and lashed out at my bruised, sensitive face.

"Steve was screaming, 'Don't touch her face!'. But the policeman didn't realise the significance. He grazed my lip and cut my cheek and then we had a massive fight.

"All reason went out of me because it was my damaged face. I'd just had one hundred stitches in my face and there was this fifteen stone guy attacking me."

Sian recalled that the judge described the case as "a storm in a teacup".

"I was only charged with kicking the policewoman, which I can't remember doing, I must have caught her when I was going for the guy!"

She later blamed, "too much German food and too much German wine". She and Steve split up shortly after the conclusion of the court case.

A year after handing over her Miss Wales crown Sian was asked by a photographer friend to pose for him as a favour. She plucked up the courage to do so, but was desperately upset, when she saw the finished pictures, to assume that he had touched them up to hide her facial scars.

She was incredulous and delighted to find out that he hadn't altered the photographs at all. "I was beautiful again!" she said.

With her stunning looks restored, Sian went on to carve an extraordinarily successful modelling career, particularly as a Page Three girl for *The Sun* newspaper, and even now she regularly makes the chart in polls to find the readers' favourite of all time.

She also appeared in the 1985 James Bond film, *A View To A Kill*, alongside fellow beauty queens Carolyn Seaward, Miss UK 1979 (one-time paramour of Prince Andrew) and Mary Stavin, Miss World 1977, a long-term girlfriend of George Best.

Sian appeared in the tabloids once again in 2007, when the *Mail on Sunday* reported on a mission by a secretive men's club in the States to track down the girl who had adorned its walls for the past 27 years.

The Bohemian Grove Club wanted to find the subject of the poster, posed for in 1980, to help them celebrate their 100th anniversary.

An internet expert identified the model as Sian and finally managed to track her down to where she now lives on Ibiza, with her Italian husband and their son and daughter.

When Sian learned of the club's obsession with her and their bid to entice her to the celebrations, she proved she'd lost none of her talent for controversy.

"Since they are so secretive, how do I know if this will be a nice gentlemen's dinner or men leaping around doing weird and distasteful things in a forest?", she said.

"This sounds like rich and famous men banning women so they can run around like Boy Scouts."

Kathy Anders

"This is better than winning the pools"

Kathy Anders, Miss England 1974

When Kathy Anders married pools heir David Moores the media nicknamed her the "Real Life Cinderella".

But, like so many fairytales before and since, the story was to have a dark underbelly that ended in tragedy.

Kathy's life had indeed encompassed all the clichés – a rags to riches tale that made her one of the most popular beauty queens of the early '70s. The daughter of a coal merchant, her childhood had been spent in an end of terrace house in the industrial town of Rochdale, Lancashire.

The girl with the Gracie Fields accent left school at 16 to work in a blanket mill and as a petrol pump attendant before she embarked on a modelling course that would change the direction of her life forever. In 1969 she won her first beauty title which paved the way to countless more, before culminating in the crowning glory of winning Miss England 1974.

She met David Moores, heir to the £300m Littlewoods Pools empire, at a modelling assignment in London and the handsome couple announced their engagement in 1971. "This is better than winning the pools", she said at the time.

Yet her rise to the top was by tortuous route. It was only at her wedding that she revealed that the man giving her away wasn't her real father. Such was the stigma of divorce in those days, Kathy concealed her parents' split in 1960 in the fear it would harm her career.

Her triumph as Miss England was an astonishing one. Twelve months earlier, to the very day, she had been battling for her life after the sports car she had been driving - a present from fiance David – overturned on the M63. Kathy had been trapped upside down for an hour before she was rescued. Her hands and face were gashed, her thigh bone broken, and she had been covered in petrol.

"The pain was so dreadful," she recalled. "I thought I'd lost my leg".

Kathy was in hospital for five months and had to use a caliper for three. At the time of the crash she was heading for the big time, but doctors told her she would never again walk without a limp.

But they reckoned without Kathy's cast-iron will to recover. She got a friend to yell at her every time she walked with a limp and spent painful hours walking up and down stairs with a book balanced on her head.

Kathy told a *Rochdale Observer* reporter in 1973 that the accident was one of the most important things that had ever happened to her.

"It really changed my outlook on life," she said. "I was on my back for a long time in hospital, just thinking I was lucky to be alive. And from then on I found things that I worried about before, didn't bother me anymore."

Kathy's single-minded determination to overcome the after-effects of this accident gave the tragedy of four years later an even more appalling irony.

She was still convalescing when she decided to enter the Blackburn heat of the Miss England contest. She said: "The only reason I entered was to boost my confidence after being out of beauty contests for a year."

Having won the heat, Kathy was back on stage and crowned Miss England live on BBC TV, exactly one year after her accident. She modestly attributed part of her success to being out of the public eye for the best part of a year.

"You see, they are always looking for new faces and having been unable to do anything for 12 months meant I wasn't in everyone's mind," she explained. In the swimsuit round, she hid the steel pin in her thigh with a carefully-placed hand.

As Miss England, Kathy made the final 12 of the Miss Universe contest, and finished second in Miss United Kingdom – pipped at the post by Helen Morgan, later to become Miss World. Kathy also finished fifth in Miss Europe in the same year.

In February 1976, she finally wed her prince. The wedding had already been delayed twice – once due to her accident, and then again to allow her to fulfil her year of duties as Miss England. The ceremony was held at the 14th century parish church in the village of Halsall, and Kathy looked stunning in a gown and headdress of antique lace, with her close friend and Miss England runner-up, Jeannie Galston, as a bridesmaid.

The couple set up home in a five-bedroom mansion with swimming pool, set in two acres of land, but neighbours from her childhood days recall that Kathy never lost sight of her roots, nor affected any airs or graces. Said one: "She never became a snob even when everyone knew she was going to marry Mr Moores. She was always 'Our Kathy'".

DAVID MOORES

I'm alone, said pools heir as wife lay trapped in crash car

Nightmare death of a beauty

The mansion they were driving back to .

By Leslie Clare

THE FULL horror of the road crash death of Kathy Anders, a Miss England who became the bride of the Littlewoods Pools heir, was revealed yesterday.

Her husband David Moores, 51, was so shocked after his Daimler somersaulted into a ditch that he forgot to tell rescuers his wife was also in the car.

And though 26-year-old Kathy suffered only minor injuries she died from inhalation of mud.

In other words she drowned in thick mud," Mr John Benstead Gordan, a Home Office pathologist, told the Ormskirk, Lancs, inquest.

Mr Moores who did not give evidence, sat with his head bowed choking back tears as the coroner learned how tragedy struck the pools family last September for the second time—only a few months after David's brother Nigel, 39, also died in a car crash.

Picturesque

On that September night David Moores was driving back with Kathy to their £300,000 mansion home called Greenacres in a picturesque village near Southport.

In a narrow lane his Daimler failed to negotiate a minor bend, and somersaulted into a ditch. It was found by another motorist, Stephen Clark.

The Daimler was in about two feet of water, but Mr Clark said he could not open the doors. They were jammed. Mr Clark added he could see only Mr Moores alone.

Sergeant Kenneth Hornby, among policemen who went to the scene, also thought Mr Moores was alone. And the sergeant said: " During the rescue operations Mr Moores kept insisting he was alone."

It was only when he was being helped away that Mr Moores said: "Get my wife. She is in there. Is she all right?"

Twenty-five minutes after the crash Kathy was brought out.

Mr Moores suffered serious head injuries and Constable Michael Barrow said that because of this he was not allowed to breathalyse him.

But the constable added that the supervisor of a discotheque where the couple had been said Mr Moores did not drink more that night.

Sensation

Mr Moores himself later told the constable that all he would remember of the accident was " a sensation of motion through the air."

Mr John Stannard, for Mr Moores said : " I do not think anyone ever suspected he was drunk."

Coroner Mr Howard McGann said there was no evidence of dangerous driving, and no criminal proceedings would be taken.

Verdict : Misadventure.

When she was Miss England... Kathy Moores in 1974

Going at £7m ... a London palace fit for a sheik

By Robert McGowan

THE ARABS have a way with money. A year ago they bought London's largest private house—for under £2,000,000. Now—with planning permission for 63 houses in the extensive grounds, plus £600,000-worth of alterations—it's up for sale again . . . for £7,000,000.

The only London home likely to cost more is Buckingham Palace.

The 63-roomed house is Witanhurst on Highgate Hill. The only people allowed in at the moment are the decorators.

A spokesman for agents Aylesford & Company, said : " We are not able to allow anybody to view the house unless they intend to buy.

'No Briton'

" We have already received one genuine inquiry."

He added : " No Briton, no American and no pop star can afford this one. About 50 people in the world have this kind of money."

The main reception room, 100ft long, opens out on to the garden which overlooks most of London. There are also massive kitchens and garaging for half a dozen cars.

The agents added : " At a conservative estimate the house could £1,000 a week or more to run."

Send a Giles this year

SEND a happy Christmas with Giles

Beaverbrook Newspapers is once again producing a series of Giles Christmas cards and a special calendar.

National Institute for the Deaf. Price is £2.99 for 20 cards and envelopes. Apply to : The Books Department, Beaverbrook Newspapers Ltd., 1 House, 35 Farringdon Street, London EC1A 4DT.

No name yet!

A Christmas christening has been planned for Princess Anne's baby. Master Phillips' name is to be revealed for at least another week or even until the christening.

Woolies joins the union

THE giant chain store Woolworth has agreed to recognise the shopworkers' union after a 16-year battle.

The decision was taken by the workers themselves . . . in a company-organised ballot.

The Union of Shop Distributive and Allied Workers—U.S.D.A.W.—will now start talks on pay and conditions for 60,000 employees.

The agreement is not for a closed shop and no pressure will be put on workers to join the union—which already has about 10,000 members in Woolworth stores.

U.S.D.A.W. made its first formal approach to Woolworth in June this year.

Glenn Miller: Mystery find

A FISHERMAN'S haul is being sent to the American Embassy in London . . . to see if it holds the key to the tragic end of the Glenn Miller story.

Skipper Brian Hills hauled in a brass plate with parts of aircraft wreckage, two miles off Newhaven, Sussex, while fishing in his trawler Wildflower.

The plate tattled an engine serial number. There was also an engraved sign with the name of the Bendix Aviation Corporation, Wayne.

The bandleader disappeared over the Channel 33 years ago while flying from England to France. Locals believe that the single-engined plane came down between Newhaven and Seaford.

Another neighbour recalled that their house was like a "little palace", adding, "My kids used to sit on the wall and look in at parties they held round their swimming pool when they entertained footballers from Liverpool, Everton and Manchester."

Kathy indulged her love of dogs by breeding and showing Great Danes – she won Best of Breed at *Crufts* – but it wasn't long before she started talking about starting a family.

Then came that fateful night in September 1977. The couple had been married for just 18 months when 32 year old Mr Moores was driving them both home from an evening out at a restaurant near Formby. His Daimler-Jaguar skidded on a bend, ploughing a 40-foot scar along a deep ditch, before somersaulting and landing upside down in the murky water.

The passenger side of the car was submerged in water.

A passer-by called firemen to the scene and they found David Moores barely conscious. He was reportedly in such shock that he forgot to tell rescuers that his wife was in the car with him.

The *Daily Express* reported that one of the policemen on the scene that night told the inquest, "During the rescue operation Mr Moores kept insisting he was alone."

It was only when he was being helped away that he said, "Get my wife. She's in there. Is she all right?"

Until then the fireman weren't aware that there was anyone else in the car. They felt around in the water and found Kathy's body beneath the surface. Attempts to revive her with oxygen failed; she had drowned in two feet of water or, as the pathologist at the inquest put it, from inhalation of thick mud.

The inquest delivered a verdict of misadventure.

At the time, the Moores dynasty – nicknamed the English Kennedys - was only just beginning to recover from another devastating tragedy. Just five months before Kathy's death, David's elder brother Nigel, a renowned playboy, had died in a car crash in France.

Kathy's brother told of their family's terrible grief at the loss of his beloved sister. "There used to be four children in our family," he said, "and now there are only three".

The Moores family asked reporters to leave them alone. A family friend said, "They have taken Kathy's death very badly".

Kathy's funeral in Southport was attended by 90 relatives and close family friends, with her ashes interned in a quiet rural graveyard. At 25 she had had everything, only for the curse of the English Kennedys to snatch it cruelly away.

David Moores recovered from the accident after hospital treatment and later remarried. He became Chairman of Liverpool FC from 1991-2007 and is now honorary Life President.

Littlewoods Pools was sold in 2002 for £750m.

Cindy Breakspeare

"People thought I was absolutely crazy"

Cindy Breakspeare, Miss World 1976

Cynthia Jean Breakspeare wasn't originally seen as a front-runner to win Miss World 1976, but a few helpful pointers along the way guided her to an unexpected victory.

Jon Osborne styled himself as Eric and Julia Morley's 'right-hand man' in the Miss World organisation for ten years in the '70s. His parting from the company at the end of that decade was a bitter one, and in his animosity he sold a series of revealing interviews to the *News of the World*, exposing what really went on behind the scenes at the world's biggest beauty contest.

One controversy he shared was the special treatment he bestowed on certain contestants, on whom he would then place a bet and often win tidy sums, despite the fact that Miss World employees were banned from betting on the event.

One contestant who caught his eye during the run-up to the 1976 contest was the aforementioned Cindy Breakspeare, Miss Jamaica.

Said Jon, "The contest wasn't fixed, but the girls we gambled on got preferential treatment. We made sure Cindy looked good and even changed her hairstyle. She didn't realise that none of the other girls were getting that sort of attention."

Cindy started out in the contest as a 50-1 outsider, and as a result of Jon's flutter, he ended the evening £5,000 richer when she won the crown.

He added. "If Eric Morley had known about my betting, he'd have sacked me on the spot."

Cindy herself would rather attribute her victory to her own natural charms. She remembers being able to pinpoint exactly when she was started to be seen as a favourite for the title.

"We all had to parade in front of the press in our swimsuits," she recalls in a TV documentary. "That's when my odds went right down".

The green-eyed brunette from the sun-kissed Caribbean isle swept the board at the final at London's Albert Hall.

Years later, she confessed that she'd gone Commando as she took her victory walk. "There simply wasn't enough time between changing from swimsuits to evening gowns to put any underwear on," she confessed.

At least one of her rival contestants was suspicious about the result. The *Daily Mirror* reported that the fourth-placed Miss Finland (a hot favourite with the bookmakers) complained afterwards that the contest may have been rigged, due to the fact that Cindy was also crowned the winner during the dress rehearsal before the live show.

Cindy dismissed the allegations without undue concern. "I think this kind of thing is highly insulting to all the judges. Other girls were also crowned at other rehearsals. Miss Finland is being unfair".

Cindy was born in Toronto, Canada, but moved to Jamaica at the age of 4. After winning the Miss Universe Bikini contest and opening her own health club, she was invited, aged 22, to represent Jamaica in the Miss World contest (the socialist government of the day had chosen to drop their official contest in protest against the apartheid regime in South Africa).

She proved to be an extremely popular Miss World with the public, but it was her choice of consort – for want of a better word – which raised more than a few eyebrows, both here and among her countrymen.

Just weeks into her reign, it was revealed that Cindy was the girlfriend of legendary reggae star Bob Marley. The affair was uncovered when the Rastafarian musician was wounded in an assault by an unidentified gunman outside the home he shared with his wife Rita in Jamaica.

Marley sustained only minor injuries, but Cindy – miles away in London – was distraught when she heard the news and, according to newspaper reports, refused to carry out her Miss World duties that evening.

The press got wind of the relationship and the headlines carried stories of, "Miss World and Her Wild Man".

The pair had met when they both lived in apartments at Hope Road, Kingston, and Bob would woo his neighbour with his music. Cindy had been living alone since the age of 18 and was, in her own words, "savvy and street-smart".

A Miss World insider who worked closely with Cindy during her reign was less than impressed with her attitude.

"Basically, at first, she didn't want to be here - she wanted to be in Jamaica with Bob Marley.

"She moaned and groaned about everything: she hated our weather, she thought we were working her too hard, she didn't like dressing up or straightening her hair for public appearances. She said Bob didn't like it and she had to make sure it was definitely frizzy again for him.

"In every Mecca establishment she visited - usually three a night - they laid on a steel band for her, but they weren't *Jamaican* steel bands so she moaned about that as well. I would say she was totally unprofessional, and consequently there were complaints about her from the Mecca regional managers.

"We had to barter with her in the end, promise her this and that to get her to carry out a job."

Cindy's attitude changed entirely once Bob Marley came to London, the insider continued. "She was all smiles then, a changed person".

The affair caused consternation further afield than just the Miss World Organisation; in Jamaica, a relationship between an uptown girl and a 'dread' – a poor Rastafarian – was seen as the ultimate taboo. Cross-social class interactions weren't just frowned upon, they were unheard of.

Says Cindy, "I have girlfriends who tell me today that their parents sat them down on the couch in the living room and said, 'Now listen, you see what Cindy has done? Don't even think about it!' It was quite outrageous!" she laughs.

In 1978 – less than nine months after handing over her crown - Cindy gave birth to Bob's son, Damien. In all, Bob fathered thirteen children with nine different women, and once boasted, "The Bible says ye shall go forth and multiply. Well, I like to think I'm doing my bit."

Cindy remembers, "Back in those days, people thought I was absolutely crazy. Absolutely crazy! Is he clean? Is his hair clean? Does he smell? And those were just some of the petty things they could find to focus on. So it was really quite outrageous. Uptown girls were not going out with Rastafarians, and they certainly were not having babies for them."

At the same time, the black community of Jamaica couldn't understand why Bob had chosen to be with a white woman.

Eighty flee monkey fever hospital

By KEVIN O'LONE

AMBULANCES evacuated eighty patients from a London hospital last night in a new deadly fever alert.

The only patient left behind in the isolation hospital was scientist Geoffrey Platt.

Laboratory tests confirmed yesterday that he is suffering from green monkey disease.

A team of four doctors and twenty-two nurses have agreed to go into voluntary quarantine with him to look after him.

The evacuation of the Coppetts Wood hospital at Muswell Hill was ordered to prevent the spread of the fever. Domestic and ancillary workers at the hospital have been given a week's paid leave.

Rare

A Department of Health spokesman said: "This disease is very rare and very new and we don't want to take any chances."

Mr. Platt, 42, who works at the secret Porton Down germ warfare centre in Wiltshire, is in a plastic isolation tent.

He caught the disease while working on imported monkeys. A syringe containing the virus pierced a protective glove he was wearing.

Last night his condition had improved slightly. His wife Eileen, 40, and their sons Richard, 11, and Graham, ten, are under quarantine at their home in Salisbury.

The family are among forty-four people who have been in contact with Mr. Platt, who will be kept under quarantine (or at least two weeks.

THE GOVERNMENT yesterday made the disease notifiable putting it in the same category as rabies, smallpox and Lassa fever.

Pot-smoking Bob's my guy says Cindy

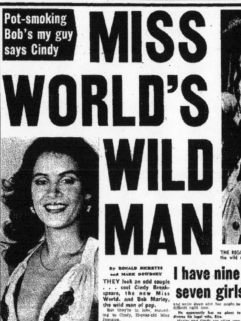

THE BEAUTY QUEEN: Miss World Cindy Breakspeare yesterday.   Picture: KENT GAVIN

MISS WORLD'S WILD MAN

THE REGGAE KING: Pop singer Bob Marley, the wild man who has a real lust for life.

By RONALD RICKETTS
and MARK DOWDNEY

THEY look an odd couple . . . cool Cindy Breakspeare, the new Miss World, and Bob Marley, the wild man of pop.

But they're in love, according to Cindy, 22-year-old Miss Jamaica.

"Bob's my boyfriend" she announced in London yesterday.

Bob, a 31-year-old Jamaican, is a reggae superstar with a cure lust for life.

He says he has fathered nine children or seven girls. He says he smokes "a pound of pot a day."

And, as a member of the fanatical Rastafarian movement he believes it is morally wrong to cut his hair.

Cindy a health-loving vegetarian, declined yesterday to divulge any details of her romance with Marley.

After the Miss World victory, she said she would like to marry and settle down with children.

But getting Marley to marry

I have nine children by seven girls, he claims

and settle down with her might be difficult right now.

He apparently has no plans to divorce his legal wife, Rita.

Marley and Cindy are often seen together in Jamaica.

The singer's manager, Don Taylor, said in New York last night: "We deal with Rita in a much more relaxed way in the Caribbean.

Vanished

"Bob loves all his kids and takes good care of his family. But he doesn't live at home much. He's a bit of a gypsy—he lives everywhere.

"I know Cindy well. Bob and Bob are good friends, but I don't know of any special relationship between them. If he was going to

get divorced, I would be the first to know."

Meanwhile Marley was lying low. A friend said in Kingston. She himself's capital: "Bob seems to have vanished from his usual haunts. I bet he's off enjoying himself somewhere."

Back in London, another Miss World contestant said that she was "suspicious" about the scandal because Cindy had been crowned the victor in a close rehearsal.

The complaint came from Miss Finland, 21-year-old Marja Helena Tammi.

But Cindy replied: "It is totally unfair to suggest that I knew I was going to win. And I think this kind of thing is highly insulting to all the judges.

"Other girls were also crowned at earlier rehearsals. I think Miss Finland was very unfair."

The relationship eventually crumbled but they stayed in close touch right up until 1981 when Marley died from skin cancer, aged just 36.

His long-suffering wife Rita stored her vitriol for Cindy for her biography of Bob, accusing the beauty queen of being "raised to pimp men with money", and deliberately positioning herself to snare her husband.

Marley's manager Don Taylor agreed with Rita in his own book, and added that he had lost all respect for Cindy when he realised that she just closed her eyes to Bob's disrespectful behaviour and numerous affairs with other women during their relationship.

Cindy, now an interior designer in her native Jamaica, went on to marry twice and have two more children. She and her second husband Rupert Bent perform together as jazz musicians, and a few years ago she hit the Jamaican pop charts with her own composition, a ballad called *Midlife Crisis*.

Today, Cindy and Rita greet each other with affection. But, the beauty queen acknowledges, "I will always be a thorn in her side".

Of Bob, she says, "People go through life idolising their role models and heroes but never knowing them. I knew mine. And I knew him well. There's no artiste in the world, no humanitarian, no freedom fighter that I look up to more than Bob. To this day that has never ceased being a privilege."

Damien "Jr Gong" Marley, her son with Bob, has followed in his father's footsteps and is now a Grammy award-winning reggae artist himself and has achieved hit singles with the likes of Gwen Stefani, Sean Paul and a collaboration with Mick Jagger. His own son was born in 2009, and he divides his time between homes in Miami and Jamaica.

Refreshing, articulate and still a beauty, Cindy remains one of the most popular winners with the public.

The girl for whom Bob Marley wrote *Turn The Lights Down Low* has nothing but good to say of her time as Miss World.

"If I had to live my life over," she said, "I certainly wouldn't leave it out."

Pamella Bordes

"£500 a night and I'm very discreet"

Pamella Bordes, Miss India 1982

Mistresses and escorts have long held newspaper editors and readers in their thrall.

The role of sexy, yet secret, concubine, desirable, yet ultimately dangerous, companion to some of the most powerful men in history, has been covered in slavish detail in books, plays and movies since time began.

These women (and occasionally men) wield enormous power, yet by their very nature must remain way down the pecking order of their partners' public persona. They can bring a man down, yet they know their place. It's a delicate balance and only the biggest risk-taker can tread the tightrope with skill.

One mistress who played her role to near perfection was Miss India 1982, the exotically beautiful Pamella Bordes, who vowed she could bring the British government down if she chose to sell her story. She revelled completely in the limelight that this intriguing mix of sex, beauty and politics brought to the late '80s.

Pamella was the lover of *The Sunday Times* editor, Andrew Neil, as well as the escort for the Minister of Sport, Colin Moynihan. What neither man knew was that she was soon to be exposed as the escort of a Libyan arms dealer and that she was working as a high-class call girl.

The story sent the media into such a frenzy that parallels were drawn between Pamella and Mati Hari, and the case was compared with the Profumo scandal of the '60s.

The former Pamella Singh Choundary had enjoyed a privileged upbringing, her father being an Officer in the Indian Army. She attended public school and studied literature at college in Delhi.

A college friend remembers, "She was embarrassingly forthright and somewhat headstrong."

According to another friend, Pamella had always sought fame and fortune.

Her first step up the ladder came when she was crowned Miss India in 1982. She took part in the Miss Universe contest in Lima, and vowed never return to village life once she had experienced such glitz and glamour.

Added the friend, "Pamella is a small-time Indian girl who discovered early on how to use and manipulate men."

Pamella moved firstly to New York, mixing in social circles that included arms dealer Adnan Khashoggi and the Emir of Qatar.

She then moved to France, where she met and married Parisian businessman Henri Bordes. The couple separated shortly afterwards and Mr Bordes later admitted that theirs was a marriage of convenience to enable his wife to escape an arranged marriage in India.

Pamella's next stop was England in 1988, where she got together with *Sunday Times* editor, Andrew Neil. She apparently told him that during the day she was taking a course in cordon bleu cookery and flower arranging. However, their stormy relationship soon made the social diary pages.

She was also photographed attending the Conservative Party's Winter Ball with Sports Minister Colin Moynihan, and spotted at events with Donald Trelford, editor of *The Observer*.

Media mogul Rupert Murdoch owned both *The Sunday Times* and *The Sun* at that time. When the more downmarket tabloid printed a photo of Pamella and Trelford, together with the headline, "I'm Not Dirty Don", the rival editor of *The Observer* was not pleased.

Trelford retorted, "It is not, you may notice, a headline saying, 'I'm Not Randy Andy', even though Mr Neil's connection is a matter of record and mine, at most, is tangential".

Tory MP Henry Bellingham was yet another gentleman rather taken with Pamella, so much so that he helped her to gain a House of Commons security pass to work as a research assistant for Dover MP, David Shaw.

But Pamella's high flying social whirl was about to suffer a setback.

A *News of the World* undercover reporter, posing as a businessman, exposed the 27 year old socialite as a high-class call girl.

"£500 And I'm Very Discreet", blazed the headlines.

Andrew Neil was so humiliated and embarrassed by this new knowledge that he ended his relationship with Pamella. The fiery Indian was outraged at his decision and, letting herself into Neil's flat in Onslow Gardens, scrawled obscenities over his mirrors, poured his single malt whiskey down the drain, and cut up six of his expensive suits and shirts.

In his 1996 autobiography, *Full Disclosure*, Neil talks of Pamella's 'violent mood swings' and that at the end of their relationship she posted 'a large piece of dog excrement' through the letterbox.

So far, so titillating, but hardly government-threatening stuff. "A Storm in a B-Cup", concluded one newspaper.

But then a friend of Pamella contacted the *London Evening Standard* with a story that would send shockwaves around the entire Houses of Parliament.

Pamella had, said the friend, been making regular trips to Paris, where she had socialised with Ahmed Gadaff Al Daim, a high-ranking major in the Libyan security service and a cousin of the feared Libyan leader, Colonel Gaddafi. It was also alleged that she had made a number of social visits to the Libyan capital, Tripoli, by private jet.

Mr Ahmed Gadaff Al Daim was already well known to Western security agencies, including Britain. A handsome 36 year-old, Mr Al Daim was a feared figure among the Libyan exile community living in Britain.

At one of Paris's most luxurious hotels, mention of Mr Al Daim's name brought a look of alarm to the manager's face.

"If you know who he is, you must understand why I do not want to say anything about him. He is a very powerful man and I do not want to get into trouble."

Asked about friends, the manager smiled and said: "He is always with beautiful girls. But he is very discreet. We never ask who they are and he certainly never tells us."

Pamella's 'friend' confirmed that she too stayed at the same hotel. Pamella would boast of her social conquests and let slip her friendship with Mr Al Daim.

With the affair now a possible matter of national security, Prime Minister Margaret Thatcher was urged to mount an immediate investigation to ascertain if Pamella was meeting Al Daim at the same time as working at the Commons and to ask how she had managed to pass a security-clearance check.

Pamella went into hiding to flee the uproar, leaving behind a bunch of squabbling newspaper editors and enough salacious gossip to keep the satirical *Private Eye* magazine in copy for months to come.

According to *Time* magazine, *The Sun*'s owner Rupert Murdoch ran a poll of British newspaper editors to find out if they too had dallied with Ms Bordes. *The Sun* had to later issue an apology to The *Mail on Sunday*'s Stewart Steven, who complained that by leaving him out of the poll, it had "impugned his manhood".

To add to the media in-fighting, Andrew Neil sued Peregrine Worsthorne for libel, and won £1,000, after the *Sunday Telegraph* editor wrote that 'playboys' should not edit newspapers. Neil later admitted that he regretted getting so "worked up" about the episode.

In his autobiography, PR supremo Max Clifford confessed that he had been the one to break the story of Pamella being a £500 a night prostitute – to deflect attention away from her Madame, a personal friend of his.

Whilst in her self-imposed purdah, Pamella went to Bali with a friend. However, the paparazzi caught up with her and, while chasing her on her moped, caused her to crash. Both she and her friend sustained injuries that later required plastic surgery.

The scandal brought huge shame on her family back in India. "She is dead to us," her grandmother told reporters. "If I had the strength I would even kill her myself." Pamella's mother agreed. "I have no daughter," she said.

Daily Mail columnist Lynda Lee Potter interviewed Pamella for the newspaper, and called her, "sickeningly self-obsessed, utterly immoral and unashamedly amoral", adding that she was "one of the most remorseless social climbers of her time".

Many years later, Pamella reflected on that period of her life. "Sometimes I made really bad decisions, trusted people who let me down. I can do without hassles in my life. I'm not going to turn round and say, 'Oh, every experience enriched me', or any such cliché. I honestly wish I hadn't met certain people. The accident with the press was horrible...".

Pamella now makes her living as a freelance photographer and is reconciled with her mother, while Andrew Neil can never escape his association with her so long as it provides mirth and titillation for his media colleagues.

As an editorial in *The Sun* concluded at the time: "If you can't stand the heat, stay out of the kitchen. And keep your hands off the tarts!"

Rosemarie Frankland

"Shove it in the archives and forget about it"

Rosemarie Frankland, Miss World 1961

The villagers of Rhos still talk amongst themselves even now about their most famous resident – the daughter of a factory worker who swept almost all before her in 1961, and lost it too. She was their very own tragic heroine in the Hollywood starlet mould.

Rosemarie and her 1974 counterpart Helen Morgan mirrored each other's beauty queen achievements exactly – both won Miss Wales, both finished second in Miss Universe, then both went on to capture the Miss UK crown before the pinnacle of their success in Miss World. She and Helen still to this day jointly hold the title of the most successful British beauty queens of all time.

American entertainer Bob Hope was part of the Miss World judging panel that night in 1961, and had the honour of crowning her as the winner. He said to the press afterwards, "She is the most beautiful girl I ever did see."

In her first interview as the new Miss World, Rosemarie was remarkably frank, and announced that she was giving up the beauty business. "Everyone thinks this is a picnic," she told the *Daily Express*. "But it's not, it's hell.

"You have to become an automaton. We walk mechanically to music, and smile to music. Hour after hour we've been rehearsing. If anyone thinks there is any glamour attached to all this, they must be crazy."

At the time of her Miss World win, Rosemarie was still living with her parents and younger sister in a council house in Lancaster. Her father was a factory worker and Rosemarie's then boyfriend, photographer Ben Jones, had proposed, she said, just before the Miss World final.

"He never wanted me to take part anyway," she added.

Although Eric Morley speaks of her, and her year's reign, glowingly in his autobiography, *The Miss World Story*, she caused concern for him just after relinquishing her crown.

Rosemarie had earned £20,000 during her year of office as Miss World – a huge sum in those days – but came sobbing into Eric Morley's office clutching a tax demand she simply couldn't pay. Don Short's 1976 book, *Miss World The Naked Truth*, recalled the dramatic episode.

"Crying won't help", Eric barked, in his inimitably forthright manner.

Fortunately for the tearful beauty, Morley had earned his reputation as a shrewd and careful businessman, and had had the foresight to invest some of her earning in shares, in preparation for such a tax demand.

Don Short wrote that Rosemarie was truly grateful, yet completely unable to account for the £20,000 she had blown in the space of a year.

After relinquishing her beauty titles, Rosemarie married Ben Jones, sixteen years her senior, in 1963 but the marriage barely lasted six months before they split, and they were later divorced on the grounds of her adultery. After they had separated, Bob Hope, then 58, took Rosemarie to Los Angeles and installed her as his "personal assistant", promising to make her a star.

She moved into his Palm Springs home and appeared in his movie, *I'll Take Sweden*. In all she appeared in five films, including the beauty queen expose, *The Beauty Jungle,* and the Beatles' hit, *A Hard Day's Night.*

Hope took her on a tour of American forces in the Arctic, joking: "She's so hot, we were in real danger of going through the ice."

However, her film career stalled and Rosemarie found herself back in her role of Hope's assistant. When Hope refused to commit to her, that position came to an end too.

In 1970 she married Warren Entner, the former guitarist of rock band Grass Roots. They had a daughter and lived in the former home of F Scott Fitzgerald in LA, but divorced ten years later.

In a 1975 interview with *Radio Times*, with accompanying pictures of her looking stunningly beautiful, Rosemarie said, "I hear dreadful things about some beauty queens now, how they are screwed up or on the verge of suicide. It shouldn't be like that."

How prophetic those words turned out to be, when her body was found at her home at Marina del Ray, LA, on 2nd December, 2000.

The cause of her death, at the age of 57, was said to be heart failure brought on by a drugs overdose. The LA rumour mill went into full swing. She was found after a week, they said, with an empty bottle of prescription pills in her hand and an empty tequila bottle nearby. Friends said she had never recovered from the fact that her secret lover of thirty years, Bob Hope, had ceased his regular payments to her three years earlier. Life didn't seem worth living anymore, she had told them.

"Hope was the only man she had ever loved," continued the friend. "Over the years he spent a fortune on her, supporting her and giving her gifts".

Rosemarie's uncle, Ray Jones, told the *Liverpool Post* that he believed it was an accident as she "would never have killed herself.

"My wife Joan and I spent a month with her in June and had already made plans for our next visit," he went on. "She seemed quite happy. I saw no evidence of drugs or excessive alcohol during the whole time we were there.

"On the night before the day on which she is presumed to have died she had been to a cinema with a friend, who tells me she was her normal self, but I have been bombarded by American newspaper reporters trying to say she committed suicide."

However, a neighbour in the Sixties block where she lived saw a very different to Rosemarie. "She had been depressed for about a year," she said. "She had fallen out with her boyfriend and her daughter. Her looks had faded and her glamorous life was behind her."

Rosemarie was the first ever British Miss World, and it is therefore ironic that she died one month after the death of Eric Morley, and two weeks after the 50th anniversary of the contest that made her name.

She held no nostalgic affection for the Miss World contest. In 1998, she told a newspaper that "beauty queens are dressed up and paraded down the catwalk just so some fellow can get a quick thrill. They should shove it in the archives and forget about it."

The ashes of Miss World 1961 were flown home to Wales to be buried at Rhos Cemetery in February 2001, in a ceremony attended by family members who still live in Wrexham today.

Her first husband, Ben Jones, a photographer, said: "Rosemarie was star-struck and I don't think she had the capacity to deal with it. For an 18-year-old behind the counter at Marks & Spencer to be thrown in the deep end of Miss World with no guidance and nobody to help her was too much. In the end it was a bit of a Marilyn Monroe story."

Gabriella Brum

"Those lying bitches made me quit"

Gabriella Brum, Miss World 1980

The 1980 Miss World contest was a milestone event for several reasons.

Firstly, it was celebrating its 30th birthday. And to herald in the new decade, Thames Television was screening the show for the first time, having wrestled the television rights from the BBC with a bid for £750,000.

It was also the first year that the Miss World brand was seen as a potential money-making venture, with sports marketing giant Mark McCormack adding it to his portfolio of big name clients.

Significantly – and this was very much seen as in defence to the growing clamour of voices demanding the end of the 'cattle market' altogether – it was the year in which Julia Morley signalled her intentions to stop the 'dumbing down' of contestants.

So for the first time, any mention of their vital statistics – 36-24-36 – was banned, while instead the emphasis was on personality and intelligence as part of the final judging.

The result? The victory of an 18 year old German blonde, who was living with a 52 year old soft porn film producer: not quite the outcome Julia had envisaged.

Julia had already had to contend with the emergence of topless photographs of Miss UK, Kim Ashfield, which had been taken a year earlier. But Julia reassured her that it made no differences to her Miss World chances; it was the full-frontal nude type of pictures that were against the rules.

But back to Miss Germany. Gabriella Brum lived in Los Angeles with 52 year old Benno Bellenbaum, whose film-making career had produced such classics as *Bed Bunnies* and *Golden Bananas*.

They had met at a party on a blind date arranged by a mutual friend. Gabriella had been a student of theatre costume design until she was expelled, for reasons she refused to elaborate on, and had then moved to California to be with Benno and to pursue a career as a model.

Even her victory at the Miss Germany contest had not been without controversy. It was claimed that the result was rigged because a friend of Benno's was on the judging panel.

Not, then, the greatest of pedigrees with which to impress the Morleys upon her arrival in London for the Miss World contest.

But ignorance is bliss, and Gabriella immediately became one of the hot favourites to win. At 6ft 1in she was the tallest contestant, and the press took a shine to the dazzling Fraulein, who was half-British on her father's side.

With a huge crowd at the Royal Albert Hall behind her, Gabriella easily took the crown.

Inevitably, one of the first questions put to her by the press was, "Do you think you won because of your beauty, or your brains?" To Julia Morley's discomfort, she replied, "Because of my beauty".

Gabriella was whisked away before she could answer their questions about the father she hadn't seen in years, and whether she had posed for nude photographs.

Benno was much more willing to talk to the press. He told *The Sun* after her victory: "That's great ... everybody will want her to work for them. I only hope she still finds time for me."

His optimism soon waned, though, as he tried to get hold of his lover. He attempted to telephone Gabriella at her London hotel three times, but the security guards refused to put him through to her. He complained that she "was like a prisoner."

Benno was offered £50,000 for nude pictures of Gabriella, but he denied any knowledge of these. "I haven't taken any", he claimed, "and even if I had I wouldn't dream of selling them."

During the first day of Gabriella's reign, she met the Lord Mayor of London and admitted to the press that Benno "wasn't too pleased" about her victory. The man himself confirmed this. "She was nearly in tears when she rang to say she'd have to stay in London for a year. We're both shocked at her winning because neither of us for a second expected it."

He added: "I wasn't really happy because I knew there would be problems. We knew her working and travelling as Miss World might affect our being together."

The press also reported how unpopular Gabriella had been with her fellow contestants, many of whom had planned to organise a petition to get the title transferred to runner-up Miss Guam. Miss USA called Gabriella "selfish and aggressive", while her room-mate Miss Austria said that "nobody liked her".

"Gabriella was the most unpopular girl in the contest", said Miss Ireland, Michelle Rocca. "I think she was very arrogant, and kept pushing herself forward all the time. She was always throwing tantrums. We all laughed when we heard her saying in a TV interview how many friends she had made among the others. It was supposed to be a personality contest, but Gabriella didn't have any".

(Michelle Rocca returned to the Miss World stage ten years later – as co-host. She also hosted the *Eurovision Song Contest*, before marrying singing legend Van Morrison).

After seventeen difficult hours of bickering, unpleasantness and media dirt-digging, Gabriella requested a meeting with Julia, whereupon she resigned as Miss World.

A news conference was held to announce Gabriella's decision, but Julia refused to elaborate on the reasons behind it, out of respect for "other people's confidences". She did say, though, that Gabriella would receive none of the prize money and that a new Miss World would be named on Monday.

The shortest-ever serving Miss World had hoped to slip out of Britain quietly, but the press had gathered at Heathrow airport for a final flurry of photographs and questions.

"Those Lying Bitches Made Me Quit", screamed *The Sun* the next day, documenting Gabriella's treatment at the hands of her fellow contestants.

Benno was delighted to hear that his lover had resigned. "She told me that being Miss World was like being in a prison cell," he said. "She wants to come home. Our love is so strong and so young and we want to be together".

A furious Julia Morley blasted Benno, calling Gabriella "a puppet on a string being manipulated by her boyfriend".

"This was clearly premeditated," she stormed to the press. "She was being controlled and was just a pawn in a game. She could've made her decision a lot earlier and disappeared with a lot more grace." Just for good measure, she added, "She is a sad, silly little girl".

Runner-up Miss Guam, Kimberly Santos, was on a plane to San Francisco and only learned the news of Gabriella's resignation when she spotted newspaper headlines at the airport.

Julia finally tracked her down and offered her the title.

Two weeks later, the official crowning ceremony took place on the island of Guam, and Kim went on to be what the Morleys called "one of the best title holders ever".

Kim later moved to London and enjoyed a brief relationship with the Morley's son, Julian, before embarking on a career first as a special police constable, and later, in what was seen as an unusual career choice for a beauty queen, a builder.

As for Benno, he and Gabriella married in 1981, but the union was short-lived, and the film producer committed suicide in 1984 at the age of 55.

Gabriella went down the tried and tested route of a *Playboy* nude photo spread and still resides in Los Angeles.

One notable fact is that since that fateful contest in 1980, not one Miss Germany advanced to the next round in the Miss World finals for the next 30 years.

Coincidence, or Julia's ultimate schadenfreude?

Ingrid Rivera

"Assault and Pepper"

Newspaper headline for Miss Puerto Rico 2008 final

A favourite question put to the contestants during their on-stage interview involves their relationship with the other girls. They might be asked, "How are things backstage? Are these contests really as bitchy as people think, or do you all get on well?"

Disappointingly, no contestant is on record to have answered in any way except positively. No, no, they insist, we all have a great time together, it's really friendly, there's no bitchiness.

So is it really true that scenes of saboteur, plotting and rivalry happen only in the movies, as in the beauty pageant satire, *Drop Dead Gorgeous*? Does the sisterhood really stick together in a contest devoted to who looks, moves and sounds the best?

Ask Miss Puerto Rico Universe 2008 and you may find her answer far closer to the truth.

The raven-haired Ingrid Marie Rivera wasn't new to the pageant scene by any means. She had won the Miss Puerto Rico World title in 2005 and had flown to China for the Miss World final with her countrymen's high hopes behind her.

She did extremely well, too, finishing in third place and also winning the Caribbean Queen of Beauty award.

When she chanced her luck at returning to the beauty queen arena – this time in the Miss Universe system - she was immediately installed as hot favourite to be crowned the island's queen in the lavish ceremony in San Juan. Beauty pageants are huge in the U.S. Caribbean and attract the sort of audience numbers that are a thing of the past in the UK. They also regularly draw boisterous audiences and accusations of rigged results.

But Ingrid didn't bank on such strength of feeling from her rivals to her return. She first noticed something amiss during the pageant preliminaries, when she touched up her make-up and changed from bikini into evening gown.

"I used a brush to do a bit of my face with powder and also to brush my chest, because it was a strapless dress," she said. "After less than a minute, I began itching, burning, redness, swollen — a horrible feeling," Ingrid told the *Today* programme during a live interview a few days after the event.

She said that the symptoms were so bad that she couldn't allow an official to touch her to pin her sash to her dress.

"One of the officials found my bathing suit and saw that it had been sprayed," she said. The substance apparently had a "Jell-O-ish consistency and colour," and was also found on her make-up brush. "It wasn't water," she said of the substance. "Water doesn't itch, doesn't burn."

Ingrid reported the incident to the pageant security guards and suggested that the substance may be pepper spray. She said she told them, "Don't tell anyone yet. I don't want the girls to know. I don't want people to feel pity for me".

"I wanted to stay focused on my main goal," she explained, "which was to win the crown".

The incident shook her faith in herself and her ability to win. "So many rocks had been put in my path — sacrifices, situations, hard, difficult times I had to go through."

On the night of the final, the itching happened again, but this time only when she put on her evening gown. "I had a rash", said Ingrid. When she came off stage, "they had to put me in cold wet towels. I had to take my dress off immediately."

She admitted afterwards that she had wavered about whether to withdraw. "At one point I thought, 'Am I a masochist?'" she recalled, her voice breaking. "But I said, 'I am with God and this is my goal, regardless of the results.'"

Ingrid struggled through the rest of the show with steely poise and when she was announced the winner of Miss Puerto Rico, her tears flowed without the help of any pepper.

But the mystery remained. Who or what had infected her clothing and make-up - and why?

There had undoubtedly been barely-concealed jealously among her 29 rivals. Not only were they aware of her previous success in Miss World, but they also considered that she had an unfair advantage in the fact that she had been a judge in the previous year's pageant.

Fellow contestant Bianca Morales confirmed that the girls were furious that such a pro should be allowed to take part.

"We more or less know the girls who were very mad about the situation. But definitely I'm not going to say any names. I think I'm going to leave it to the investigation and sooner or later we'll know. Everybody's going to know," Bianca told the *Good Morning America* programme.

Also speaking on the programme was former Miss America, Leanza Cornett, who said, "I know these people exist...but this level of sabotage is, I would say, absolutely unusual at this level of competition."

Organisers called it a "vile act" pulled off "from inside".

Ingrid turned over her evening gown and make-up brushes to police after the contest for forensic investigation, and the affair made the news all over the world, proving that everybody loves a bit of foul play. (Best headline: "Ingrid wins...by an itch").

She also claimed that her bag, clothes and credit card were stolen during the event. San Juan police announced they would be interviewing up to 15 people connected with the event.

However, the engrossing 'whodunnit' soon deteriorated into more of a red herring. Investigators claimed that they were skeptical that pepper spray had been involved, while a number of the contestants wondered why Ingrid's skin had displayed no redness or swelling while she was on stage. They also wondered how she could remain so composed while parading, yet crying in pain as soon as she was backstage again.

The forensic report was also unable to substantiate Ingrid's claims. Both her evening gown and make-up brushes tested negative for pepper spray. There was talk of further tests for caustic materials of her swimwear and even of using lie-detector tests on those who were present on the night of the contest.

Ingrid insisted on the *Today* programme that she hadn't been imagining it. "It's not a nervous reaction. It's not made up. It's a beauty pageant, why would I do that to myself?"

But with no proof or evidence, Ingrid's claims were on shaky ground. Could this be the first ever incident of self-sabotage in a beauty contest, or simply the result of an over-active imagination?

The question got the US buzzing. Contestant Iris Campos posted a comment on the *Today* programme blog saying, "I'm convinced the story is a lie to generate publicity for her. This story is a smoke screen for the real story, how she was unfairly favoured from day one because of her close personal friendship with the owner of the pageant. This is the real story and the real scandal".

Then American *People* magazine broke with the news that San Juan police were preparing to arrest two of the employees connected with the pageant – allegedly the pageant's security director and the catwalk coordinator. Both were said to have backed one of Ingrid's rivals, and both would be charged with assault. (Best headline: "Assault and Pepper").

But just as Miss Marple was about to deliver her verdict, Puerto Rico's top police official dashed our hopes. "It's an extremely weak case", he warned, saying that they still lacked any evidence with which to charge anyone.

Ingrid's detractors must've been enormously satisfied when she failed to advance to the final 15 in the Miss Universe pageant in Vietnam, much to the shock of the media and fans covering the event, and indeed to Ingrid herself.

But she can take comfort from the words of sympathiser Miss Teen Eastern Shore 2007, who said that "things seem OK on stage but behind the scenes it's a battle." If anyone was in doubt she added, "Last year a friend offered to iron my interview suit and scorched it. That's how bad things get, anything anyone can do to keep you from winning they will."

And that's all we really want to hear. Let the foul play re-commence!

Shannon Marketic

"I was held as a sex slave"

Shannon Marketic, Miss USA 1992

Feminists have long drawn parallels between beauty queens and the 'oldest profession in the world'. They compare the parading of semi-clad bodies in front of a panel of ogling judges, in the hope of winning money and career advancement, with the trade of the prostitute, and find little difference – except the latter profession is at least, they say, honest in its intention.

Shannon Marketic never wanted to be seen in that light, nor did she see any reason why an all-expenses paid trip to the Kingdom of Brunei should see her return with her reputation in tatters.

Nor would the Sultan of Brunei have imagined that the trip would result in his being slapped with a $90 million lawsuit and accused of allegations which, he told his countrymen, were "worse than murder".

In retrospect, it would be too easy to say that Shannon and her fellow travellers were naïve in the extreme. A total of seven women were to be paid $21,000 a week each for a trip to Brunei, to carry out 'personal appearances and promotional work', as well as holding 'intellectual conversations' with the visiting guests of the ruling family.

No alarm bells apparently went off for any of the women when they were also advised by the organising agency, to "mix with the guests in the evening and dress sexily".

Shannon LaRhea Marketic was 26 years old at the time of the Brunei controversy, but only 18 when she made her way into beauty pageants. The statuesque blonde, of Croatian descent, was crowned Miss Teen Arizona 1989, but held the title for barely a week when it was discovered that an error had been made, and she had been placed only first runner-up.

Next time round, in 1992, there was no doubt that she was the correct and true winner of the Miss California USA title, representing Los Angeles.

Whilst representing her state in the Miss USA pageant, she only just scraped into the semi-finals with the lowest score of the eleven contestants selected. It was therefore all the more extraordinary that she recovered in the judging to go on and win the overall title.

Her luck ran out in the Miss Universe pageant and she finished only 8th.

A devout Christian, she became a front woman for several religious organisations, and also found herself in great demand for TV, acting and modelling work.

When a film role she had been offered fell through, Shannon found herself unexpectedly out of work and with no regular income.

Which is how, in 1997, she found herself in possession of a return ticket to Brunei, courtesy of the Kaliber Talent Agency of LA. The offer looked too good to be true: first-class transportation to the tiny, oil-rich nation, accommodation, and $3,000 a day, in exchange, she was told, for nothing more than carrying out modelling and promotional work. She even asked her father, she said, to take a look at the contract, and he agreed it looked completely straightforward.

For Shannon and the six other women contracted for the assignment, including her friend Brandi Sherwood, Miss USA 1997, and former Miss UK finalist Paula Bradbury, it seemed a trip of a lifetime.

What followed was, indeed, a trip of a lifetime, but hardly in the way she had envisaged. In her lawsuit, Shannon claimed that she and the other women were held as 'sex slaves' and 'intimidated and coerced into performing physically and morally repulsive acts of prostitution'.

They were, she said, ordered to dance for six hours a night at parties, during which they were subjected to being groped and grabbed by the male guests. Shannon said she suffered verbal abuse and that her every movement was captured by surveillance camera.

One of men, she claimed, yelled, "I don't know why the boss paid so much money for you. You are the worst group of whores we have had over here."

Interviewed on US magazine show *20/20*, Shannon said that after 32 days of being held against her will in Brunei, she was able to smuggle a letter out to the US Embassy via a coded message to her father. Shortly afterwards, she was given two hours to pack and leave. She flew back to the US alone, having allegedly been paid just $10,000 by the agency – far short of the $97,000 owed to her.

Once home and safe, she took legal advice and the lawsuit against Sultan Hassanal Bolkiah, the world's richest man, was issued. The lawsuit used terms such as 'white slavery' and 'human chattel', but she conceded that she was not raped, nor did she have sex with anyone.

Nevertheless, the Malibu model was suing the Sultanate, and the Kaliber Talent Agency, for 'mental anguish, nightmares, difficulty sleeping, other trauma'. Importantly, Shannon admitted she had never actually met the Sultan, nor his brother, but the incidents all took place within his palace and in the company of his guests.

In total, she sought $10m in damages. "The Sultan doesn't have to answer to me," she told *People* magazine. "But he does have to answer to God."

The scandal was a huge embarrassment to the Sultan, who had only recently celebrated his 50th birthday with the likes of Prince Charles and Michael Jackson.

The Independent newspaper reported that during the Muslim festival of Eid al-Adha, the Feast of Sacrifice, the Sultan made a radio address to his 300,000 subjects.

"We have been implicated by slander and defamation that could very well undermine the respect and trust the people have placed in us," he warned. The allegations made against the sultanate, he said, were "worse than murder".

However, the Sultan was able to claim diplomatic immunity, being exempt from US jurisdiction as head of a foreign state, while his brother Prince Jefri claimed he held a diplomatic passport. The Kaliber Talent Agency was unable to deny that the Sultanate was its client, but claimed it was protected by a clause in Shannon's contract binding the parties in any dispute to outside arbitration, and not the courts.

During the court case, the opposing lawyers were scornful of Shannon's Christian image, saying that she was accompanied by 'Biblical-type gospel people'. Her own lawyers were only too happy to show off her glossy brochure, proclaiming that her most requested speaking topics included, 'How to live a Godly life', and 'Submit (to God) to Succeed'.

The tabloid press were damning of both sides in the sorry saga, bringing up the Sultan's playboy past, and asking why, if Shannon was so saintly, did she get involved in this at all, particularly when closer inspection of Kaliber's contract stated wording such as: 'All birthday money is your own. All bonus money/shopping is your own. All jewellery is your own'.

An American judge dismissed the case in March 1998, stating the Foreign Sovereign Immunity Act. During the investigations, however, it had been discovered that Prince Jefri had been spending $250 million a year importing 'models' to Brunei. His construction company collapsed a year later, with debts of $15 billion.

Shannon moved to Dallas and continued her career as a popular public speaker. In 2007, she was the star attraction at the 'Celebrate Jesus!' event in Maryland, billed as 'An Evening of Faith & Forgiveness'.

"Shannon talks about abstinence and following your dreams!", the programme announced proudly.

There was little talk of abstinence just days later when she was arrested at Dallas Fort Worth airport on a public intoxication charge.

The beauty queen claimed that she had been sober and that the police had refused to give her a breathalyser test.

In one of those beautiful ironies, Shannon was en route to Washington DC to address people with addictive behaviours.

Three years later she was arrested for shoplifting from a drugstore in Texas, despite swearing "on a stack of Bibles" that she hadn't meant to leave without paying.

Now settled in Dallas with adopted daughter, MaryDale, Shannon is still active in the Christian Church.

One of her Facebook posts aptly reads, "Sometimes God redeems your story by surrounding you with people who need to hear about your past so it doesn't become their future."

Miss France

"This imbecilic rumour was started by a deranged individual"

Genevieve de Fontenay, President Miss France Organisation

Genevieve de Fontenay is the Julia Morley of France. There are some notable similarities between the two women. While Ms de Fontenay is older than her British counterpart (she was born in 1932), they are both former models, have both presided over their respective pageants for decades with their husbands, both took over the reins when widowed, and both are assisted by their sons.

And, most pertinently, both have reputations that prove they're not to be messed with.

However, unlike Mrs Morley, Ms de Fontenay is a national institution in France, lauded for her flamboyant hats and power suits. She was awarded the Medal of Merit in 2002 and even has her own fan club.

The formidable grande dame of the Miss France pageant, she presided over the event with a rod of steel since 1953, despite selling the brand to TV production company Endemol in 2002. Her website gushes that she is "tireless, enthusiastic, friendly, funny and exemplary".

"Friendly" isn't a quality that Miss France 2008 would've chosen as an adjective to describe her new boss. Nor was there a great deal of laughter when controversial pictures of the new winner reached the attention of the woman nicknamed, due to her omnipresent head wear, *la Dame au Chapeau* - the lady with the hat.

The inhabitants of the Indian Ocean island of La Réunion were dancing in the streets when 22 year old Valerie Begue won the title of Miss France. The island is legally part of France, and Ms Begue, its first winner in three decades, became an instant heroine when she returned home to a huge welcome.

But trouble was brewing when a French magazine, *Entrevue*, published risqué photographs of Ms Begue which she had posed for three years earlier.

One depicted her licking yogurt off a concrete ledge, a second showed her floating in a swimming pool attached to a wooden cross in crucifixion pose, and another exposing her breasts.

As all entrants are required to sign a disclaimer before the contest stating that they had never posed for nude or compromising photos, Ms Begue felt the full force of Ms de Fontenay's wrath.

"If she had some courage and a bit of dignity she would say: 'I'm resigning because I'm not worthy to carry on as Miss France'", Ms de Fontenay stormed. "I wouldn't want to be seen touring the provinces with a girl like that. Let her stay in La Réunion."

Ms de Fontenay hadn't reckoned on the loyalty and pride of La Réunion's 800,000 inhabitants however. As their beleaguered beauty queen sobbed, "I made an error of youth, I admit that. But I've been betrayed", rebel forces were gathering in the Indian Ocean.

Politicians and churchmen leapt to her defence, accusing Ms de Fontenay of racism. Radio Free Dom, the main station on the island, said that it had received unprecedented telephone calls from indignant listeners. Hundreds of supporters marched through Saint-Denis, the capital, in protest and a gathering of recent Miss Réunion winners staged a demonstration. Support also came from the island MPs, and president of the Réunion Département Council.

The leader of the Roman Catholic Church on the island also backed Ms Bègue. He acknowledged that the pictures were "insulting" to Christians, but said: "Valérie is a victim who needs support. It is not up to me to pardon her, she has not offended me."

The bishop also highlighted Ms de Fontenay's hypocrisy and double standards, having paraded the contestants wearing bikinis and angel wings during the show, which he said was also a "perversion of a religious symbol".

In the face of such unprecedented protest, and with her own popularity to protect, Ms de Fontenay backed down.

"We felt that, as she had been elected in front of nine million television viewers, faced with a public that had never seen the photographs, we couldn't take the title from her," she told a news conference in Paris.

The jubilant beauty queen didn't get things all her way, though. As a compromise, Ms Begue was told she wouldn't be able to compete in the Miss Universe and Miss World pageants – both part of her prize – and would instead be replaced there by the third-placed Miss Pays de Loire, the runner-up having declined to take over.

Other Miss France winners haven't been quite so lucky. Ms de Fontenay suspended Laeticia Bleger, the 2004 victor, for six months, after photographs of her appeared in *Playboy*, while the winner in 1983, Isabelle Turpeaut, lost her crown altogether courtesy of revealing snaps in *Paris Match*.

Miss France 2001 made the headlines for a very different reason. Malicious internet gossip accused trainee nurse Elodie Gossuin of being a man, suggesting she was a post-operative transsexual. Despite the lack of any proof whatsoever, the story made its way first into US newspapers and then further afield, with poor Elodie becoming the butt of jokes and even more prefabricated tales.

The international coverage served to only substantiate such wild rumours, and Elodie's parents had no choice but to release her birth certificate and photographs of her as a child.

Ms de Fontenay charged in. "I'm terrified of this sort of media," she raged, referring to the power of the internet. "You can't stop it. This imbecilic rumour, which undermines the dignity of Elodie Gossuin, was started by a deranged individual," she stormed.

When Elodie shortly afterwards flew out to Puerto Rico to represent France in the Miss Universe pageant, the story reached its zenith. A spokesman for the pageant was quoted as saying, "Our regulations say that all delegates must be natural-born females. If she turns out to be a man, we'll put her on the first plane to France."

After suffering the indignity of much 'checking' by Miss Universe officials, Eloise was declared a 100% natural woman. And top French satirist Frederic Royer admitted he'd made the rumour up as a joke.

Justice for Eloise was seen to be done in the best possible way. Not only did she make the top 10 in the Miss Universe pageant that had originally doubted her sex, but at the end of the same year she was crowned Miss Europe 2002 in the Lebanon, which she declared "a revenge on the vicious rumours".

The lovely Eloise went on to enjoy both a political and TV presenting career in France and is now married with a baby daughter.

As for Ms de Fontenay, she resigned from the Miss France committee in 2010, after accusing new owners Endemol of failing to maintain the good taste and traditional values she claimed were hallmarks of the show.

In retaliation, she set up a rival competition, Miss Nationale, and was swiftly taken to court by Endemol in breach of the non-competition clause, as well as by an organisation claiming to hold copyright of the Miss Nationale name.

La Dame au Chapeau made her peace with both bodies, and the newly-named Miss Prestige Nationale contest is now in its fourth year.

Alicia Macado

"I'm going to eat, eat, eat!"

Alicia Macado, Miss Universe 1996

Of all the reasons to threaten to fire a beauty queen, overeating is rarely one of them.

But more than once a young girl, who has spent months dieting, training and exercising to be pageant perfect, finds her iron will dissolving the moment she lands the crown. The contest is over, she's won – it's time to let go and live a little.

This was the philosophy of one of the most engaging Miss Universe winners of recent times, the delightful Alicia Macado.

Venezuela in the mid '90s was in the grip of pageant fever. The national contest was, and still is, run with military efficiency by one Osmel Sousa, President of the Miss Venezuela Organisation since 1981 and heavily involved in the pageant since he joined the committee in 1969.

Nicknamed a 'Modern Pygmalion', Sousa specialises in the training of his pageant winners to the highest standard possible in readiness for international competition, using whatever means he feels appropriate or necessary, including plastic surgery, fitness training, dermatology and dental work.

When asked what his interpretation of the 'perfect beauty' was, he replied, "The one that doesn't exist".

Out of this living doll factory came a succession of triumphs for Venezuelan girls, winning the Miss Universe, Miss World or Miss International crowns no less than nineteen times. It is the country's national sport, and the shame of a contestant not making the top three of a pageant is almost unthinkable.

Such is the desperation of young women to capture the fame and fortune awaiting the winner of Miss Venezuela, they will go to every length to prepare. A 2014 documentary screened on BBC3 - *Extreme Beauty Queens* - followed a group of girls as they trained for Sousa's 'bootcamp', and showed one girl sewing mesh onto her tongue to prevent her from eating solid foods, and thereby aiding weight loss.

When one contestant fainted during training, Osmel was seen to bark, "If you faint like a beauty queen, get up like one".

He later said to the documentary host, "If a girl needs a nose job, you get her one. It's an industry, so we strive for perfection. We can't settle for mediocrity."

One of Sousa's most successful years was 1996, with his Miss Venezuela queens winning both Miss World and, in the shape of Alicia Macado, Miss Universe.

Once a candidate has won a heat of the Miss Venezuela contest, she begins an intensive training programme which can last for six months. She receives coaching in speech, physical fitness, make-up, modelling and all the skills required for competition. As the broadcast of the contest lasts up to four hours, with countless musical numbers and dances, rehearsals require weeks of preparation.

The winners chosen to represent Venezuela in the major pageants then undergo more preparation before they compete internationally. These efforts are funded by corporate sponsors like Pepsi, Palmolive and Colgate, attracted to the pageant by its high ratings and public profile.

Honey blonde Alicia, the daughter of a Cuban father and Spanish mother, made it through months of intensive training and self-deprivation to win the 1996 Miss Universe crown.

With the pressure off, little wonder she declared, straight after her victory, that she was going to, "Eat, eat, eat!"

And eat she did. When pictures of Alicia attending to her official duties were published showing her bloated and forty pounds heavier than on her crowning night, the ramifications were serious.

As part of her contract, Alicia had recorded an advert for Kellogg's. However, as the weight piled on, the cereal company dropped her quicker than a scalding Pop Tart. The message was clear – fat doesn't sell, especially from Miss Universe.

At first, her weight gain was dismissed as being the result of painful dental surgery. But soon it became undeniably obvious and into the fray stepped heavyweight Miss Universe owner Donald Trump. It was his first year as owner of the Miss Universe pageant and he fully intended to make his mark.

If she didn't lose weight, he threatened, she would lose her crown. With a grave lack of gallantry, while calling in live on the Howard Stern radio show to promote the 1997 Miss Universe pageant, Trump called Alicia an "eating machine".

This sparked much public debate in the States, where image and the quest for thinness is everything. Trump maintained that Miss Universe has an image to adhere to and if standards are dropped, she must face the consequences. The winner, he said, has an "obligation to stay in a perfect physical shape".

He put Alicia under a strict dieting regime and organised a photo-shoot in which she worked out in front of the press. The excess pounds started to melt away.

However, the hungry beauty queen's cage had been well and truly rattled by Trump's attitude towards her. She went onto a chat show to complain how humiliated she had been by being forced to diet and to take exercise in front of photographers. She also later complained that the organization had cheated her out of her prize money (a claim never substantiated).

It was a slimmer Alicia who appeared on stage to crown her successor, but undoubtedly a bitter one. Footage shows her practically throwing the crown at the new queen before stomping off stage.

She then gave an interview in which she said, "I'm no longer Miss Universe. I can look like a truck if I like".

Alicia went on to date singer Enrique Inglesias for a short period, to much tabloid fanfare. When asked to substantiate rumours that she had also been romanced by Donald Trump himself, she denied it emphatically, adding, "It's not because he's old – it's because his manner of being is loathsome."

Most controversially of all, two years after her reign, and by then a popular soap star, she was implicated in a cover-up of an attempted murder case.

Her boyfriend at the time, Juan Rodriguez, was accused of shooting his brother in law in the head, causing permanent brain damage. Alicia was charged with driving her boyfriend away from the scene of the crime. She denied the charges, insisting she was away filming scenes for the soap opera at the time. A judge in Caracas decided there were insufficient grounds for prosecution and the case against her was dropped.

Alicia was by then a household name in Latin America, but still found opportunities to shock. During the filming of a Mexican reality show called *La Granja* (The Farm), she was shown having sex with another contestant, leading to her then fiancé, New York Yankees' right fielder Bobby Abreu, to break off their engagement.

In 2006, she became the first Miss Universe to ever pose nude for *Playboy* and, in a delightfully sarcastic touch, she dedicated the pictures to her nemesis, Donald Trump.

In 2010 she made BBC World headlines by announcing she was forced to close her Twitter account after tweeting her hopes for "peace between the two Chinas" – her reference to the feuds between North and South Korea. "I now have a lot of psychopaths on my account, so it's best to close it and start another," she said of the gaff, which led to a stream of insults by followers.

Alicia now lives in Mexico City and continues her TV presenting and acting career, having given birth to daughter Dinorah in 2008. Shortly after the birth, she issued a statement quoting that the baby's father was Mexican businessman Rafael Hernandez Linares and not, according to respected Mexican news sources, an infamous drugs lord called Gerardo Alvarez Vazquez.

But back to the end of Alicia's tumultuous reign. In the 1997 Miss Universe pageant to find Alicia's successor, the three remaining finalists were all asked, in the traditional Final Question round, what they would choose if they could do anything for 24 hours without consequence.

In an undeniably cute reference to the controversy of the past year, Miss USA, Brook Lee, answered, "I would eat everything in the world! You do not understand me – I would eat everything TWICE!"

She won the Miss Universe title – and stayed skinny.

Nicola Willoughby

"I really regret what I did"

Nicola Willoughby, Miss United Kingdom 1999

Nicola Willoughby carries the distinction of being the last ever winner of the Miss United Kingdom title.

To fans of devolution in the UK, the addition in 2000 of separate contestants from England, Scotland, Wales and Northern Ireland in Miss World was seen only as a good thing.

It was certainly excellent news for Julia Morley; the presence of four, rather than just one, British girl, helped swell the numbers of Miss World finalists to nearly one hundred that year, beating her Miss Universe counterparts hands down (the American pageant struggles to attract more than eighty delegates most years).

Eric Morley sadly didn't live to see the four countries of the UK competing for the first time, dying just days before the 50th anniversary contest in 2000.

To those who loved the annual Miss United Kingdom contest, its demise hit them hard. No longer would they see Miss Swindon compete with Miss Glasgow, or Miss Cardiff go into battle with Miss Worksop. It was the end of an era.

Until 1999, the winners of the separate contests to find Miss England, Scotland, Wales and Northern Ireland would compete in Miss UK, along with a few dozen winners of regional heats held across the country.

The contest made for a pleasing BBC – and, from 1980, ITV - spectacle in the late summer, held for decades in the seaside town of Blackpool, before moving to London in its twilight years.

It was in the Grand Room of the Grosvenor House Hotel, London, where Nicola Willoughby made history by winning the last ever Miss UK contest proper.

The 18 year old blonde was working as an assistant in a nursing home in her hometown of Spalding, Lincolnshire, when one of her elderly patients spotted a magazine article calling for entrants for a contest to find Miss Take a Break.

The lady persuaded Nicola to send off a photo and application form.

When it decided to hold its own beauty contest for its readers in 1999, it was *Take a Break* magazine's first and only foray into the pageant world. The winner would be chosen in a proper final and go forward to the Miss UK contest later in the year.

The move proved extremely popular. Hundreds of readers sent in photos, and the magazine devoted pages to not only their own contest, but to the Miss UK finals as well.

It was Nicola's first beauty contest and in winning Miss Take a Break she beat many of the professionals who had been doing the pageant rounds for years.

Mere months later she triumphed at the Miss UK finals, courtesy of a panel of judges which included boxer Frank Bruno and entertainer Jeremy Beadle.

In some quarters it was seen as highly convenient that Miss Take a Break should go on and win Miss UK, given all the mutual publicity and back-slapping.

But it was churlish talk, as Nicola was a beauty by anyone's standards. Unlike many of her ultra-glossy predecessors, she was a naturally fresh-faced, blue-eyed blonde with a figure to die for. As soon as she was crowned, she was excitedly talked about as Britain's best hope to win the Miss World title for years.

Nicola had two further advantages. The first was that Channel 5 was screening the Miss World contest in the UK for the second year running. No terrestrial British TV station would touch the contest since 1989, so to be back in the mainstream was a huge coup for Eric Morley, who had been desperate to be accepted again.

Secondly, not only was it being screened in the UK, but it was being held in the UK too, for the first time since 1990.

The days of the Royal Albert Hall being Miss World's spiritual home were long gone. Not only had it been hounded off British TV, it had been banished from Britain itself, visiting more welcoming destinations – among them the USA, Hong Kong, the Seychelles, Sun City in South Africa, India and, later, China, Poland and Indonesia.

So the forecast for Nicola couldn't have been better – a genuinely beautiful girl (who worked with the elderly too!), a home match at London's Olympia, and live screening on prime-time TV. She looked unstoppable.

Until a tabloid newspaper spoilt the party and published photographs of Nicola modelling topless in her pre-pageant days.

Even as a new millennium approached, such lack of decorum still caused an outcry in many of the competing countries.

Suddenly, Nicola's eligibility to compete in Miss World was thrown into doubt. Julia Morley was faced with a no-win situation and found herself with a considerable dilemma.

Miss Bosnia had already withdrawn due to the revelation of a *Playboy* photoshoot, but Nicola's less explicit photos didn't appear to be quite as controversial.

When topless photos of Miss UK 1980, Kim Ashfield, appeared in the tabloids days before that year's Miss World contest, Julia had brushed the matter aside; there had been no question of Kim withdrawing.

But this was supposed to be a whole new shiny era for Miss World and, here it was, being cast back into the mire of sleaze and controversy that had tarnished it in the first place.

Nicola was understandably distraught, not just over the expose of the photos, but at the sentence hanging over her. "I really regret what I did," she cried, "I was just young". (The photos had actually only been taken eight months previously).

She pleaded for clemency and said she'd been "duped" into posing for the photos as she had attempted to break into modelling.

Nicola was keen to point out how supportive her fellow contestants were being towards her, no doubt unaware that copies of the offending newspaper pictures were being gleefully and surreptitiously swapped among her Miss World rivals, passed under the table at mealtimes.

The press then had the sheer audacity to launch a *Save Our Nicola* appeal, having orchestrated her downfall in the first place. The air inside Julia Morley's office was blue.

But what finally saved Nicola's bacon, and her place in the contest, was the demands of Channel 5.

What was the point, they asked, of screening the contest to a British audience if there was no Miss UK for them to follow and root for? The TV executives were revolting and, as ever, the power of the media forced Julia's hand.

Nicola was reinstated and, as a bonus, described by Julia as "a lovely person".

"I'm so glad to have been given the chance to represent my country," she said when told of the good news. "I'm a patriot and think this is an important thing to do."

One will never know for sure if Nicola's failure to make the final 15 was a decision made by the judges purely on merit, or as a result of the adverse publicity. But the crown pointedly went to the above-reproof Miss India, Yukta Mookhey, who spoke about spiritual healing and Godliness in her interview, and wore a dress that went right up to her neck.

A year later, a former boyfriend of Nicola's sold his story to *The People* newspaper ("My Miss United Kink-dom") telling of his "marathon eight times a night sex games" with his then girlfriend.

Having publicly spoken of her regret in posing topless, she changed her mind and, in a career move seen as the modern equivalent of becoming a Page Three girl, she modelled for a six-page set of stunning but risqué photos for *FHM* magazine.

Their readers – a million miles away from those of *Take a Break* – were impressed, and Nicola became the first Miss UK to make the Top 100 in their World's Sexiest Women annual poll.

Nicola still lives in Lincoln, where she opened her own modelling agency in 2014, and is married with two young sons.

As for that long-lost and lamented Miss United Kingdom title, it is now bestowed on the home girl who does best in the Miss World contest, and announced at the Coronation Ball after the event.

Nigeria 2002

"They will be wearing swimsuits dripping with blood"

Broadcaster Muriel Gray, on Miss World 2002

For all that Julia Morley has done for the Miss World contest, both before and after taking the reins from Eric, moving the bandwagon to Nigeria will never be hailed as her finest hour.

The episode that caused loss of life and rioting on a huge scale will go down as the darkest moment in the history of the contest.

It must've seemed such a good idea at the time. A year earlier, Nigeria's Agbani Darego became the first black African to win the title, and the government of Nigeria, caught up in the euphoria, signalled its eagerness to host the contest in 2002. What an opportunity, they thought, to boost Nigeria's tourist trade and overall image, to see it safely into the new dawn of the 21st century.

Julia too saw only positives, as well as the kudos of opening new frontiers to take the pageant where no major beauty contest had ever considered going before.

But even before the contestants set foot in the country, the protests began. Human rights advocates called for an international boycott of the contest in protest of the treatment of women in many northern Nigerian states under the law of Sharia. Under this law, a 30 year old Muslim Nigerian woman, Amina Lawal, was sentenced to death by stoning for adultery and was awaiting her fate.

A number of contestants took the decision to withdraw from the contest in support of the woman, including Miss France, who said: "When a woman faces the most agonising death, there are more important things in life than winning a crown for being beautiful."

While human rights activists applauded their decision, Julia, faced with a possible mass walkout of her girls, was clearly rattled. "This is a situation we have never come across before", she told one reporter. She was in discussions with Nigerian ministers, she said, and would monitor the situation.

The contestants had gathered in London before flying out to Nigeria, and were due to meet Prince Edward at a reception for the presentation of a cheque from the Miss World Organisation for one of his charities. However, in the face of the growing turmoil, Prince Edward cancelled the engagement.

Under this intense international scrutiny and outrage, the Nigerian government bowed to pressure and promised to revoke the sentence on Amina Lawal (which it duly did, in February 2004).

However, many Muslims were already disgruntled at the idea of a spectacle they considered offensive and indecent being held in their country. Even when Julia agreed to postpone the contest until after the holy month of Ramadan, the message was clear – we don't want you here, Miss World.

Who knows whether the show would have gone on even then? What was for certain was that not even Julia could've envisaged the sheer destruction caused by a few printed words.

A 21 year old Nigerian journalist, Isioma Daniel, was commissioned to write a piece about Miss World for daily paper *This Day*. She wrote, "What would Mohammed think? In all honesty, he would probably have chosen a wife from among them."

Many Muslims were grossly offended at this slur on their Prophet and it led to carnage. A local newspaper office in Kaduna, a northern city with a history of Muslim-Christian violence, was burnt down. Angry mobs razed churches and mosques and rampaged through the streets, looting cars, smashing shop windows and murdering bystanders in their path. The riots quickly spread to the capital Abuja, where the contest was due to be held. The Red Cross in Nigeria reported that an estimated death toll recorded at least 250, with over 1,000 more injured and 12,000 left homeless.

In the midst of these terrible scenes, the Miss World contestants were under armed guard in their hotel in Abuja. The BBC made phone contact with Miss Scotland, Paula Murphy, at the hotel, who said that they could see smoke from their bedroom windows and that everyone was "simply terrified".

The British television crew due to fly out to film the contest was also reluctant to leave the UK. The Executive Producer revealed that a girlfriend of one his team had even burned his passport to force him to stay in England.

Despite pleas from the Nigerian government to stay, Julia made the only decision she could – she got her and the girls the hell out. According to an in-depth report on the incident in *Vanity Fair*, she ordered a jet from Cameroon – costing her $400,000 – and, to huge cheers, they boarded a plane back to Britain.

As the flight touched down and the contestants were installed in a hotel at London Heathrow, their troubles were far from over.

There were calls for Julia to scrap the contest altogether. Broadcaster Muriel Gray declared that "these girls will be wearing swimsuits dripping with blood". Mayor of London Ken Livingstone blamed the contest for bringing "tragedy and strife" to Africa and said that it wasn't welcome in the capital, while Labour MP and former actress Glenda Jackson said, "They should call the whole thing off as a mark of respect to the people who died. What's the point of such a contest anyway? Miss World has become utterly irrelevant".

Novelist Kathy Lette called it "a cargo of nuclear waste which circles the world looking for a safe harbour and is shunned by all".

Julia Morley was caught on the defensive. Miss World, she said, had been used as a 'political football' and she refused to take any responsibility. Interviewed on the BBC's *Breakfast with Frost*, she blamed, "the unfortunate journalist who wrote the unfortunate article". With her trademark twisted logic she said that they weren't responsible for the deaths in Nigeria, "nor could we possibly be when Northern Ireland was fighting and we had the shows in London".

She had earlier provided another gem for the media: "To tell you the truth, before I left I thought Sharia was a girl's name," she said in the interview with *Vanity Fair*.

After Julia threatened to hold the contest in a tent in Hyde Park if necessary, Alexandra Palace, the nineteenth-century venue in north London, was booked for the final on 9th December.

By this stage, nobody really cared who won or not, but it seemed apt when the victor turned out to be a Muslim. Miss Turkey, 21 year old Azra Akin, a model, was born in the Netherlands and raised by Turkish parents, and gave the *Mail on Sunday* its glorious headline: "It's Turkey for Christmas".

The whole sorry story cost the organisation dear. Apart from the cost of chartering the plane and paying for the new venue in the UK, the money paid to the Miss World Organisation for staging the show in Nigeria was lost. The organisation's Financial Director, Michael Macario, told *Vanity Fair*, "We lost about £1m. In a good year we expect to produce £1m profit." But he added that he didn't think Julia would have to sell her home in Dulwich. "It isn't necessary at this moment in time".

Julia was devastated at the vitriol and scorn the media poured upon her. "I'm not blaming anyone else, mind you", she said. "I blame only myself. I'm the asshole here. But I only had a year in which to learn!"

The repercussions went on. A year later, Channel 4's *Cutting Edge* series screened *Beauty Queens and Bloodshed*, an expose that documented the inside story of the events of that calamitous month in which Julia Morley's behaviour was described by a *Guardian* journalist as "reckless idiocy fuelled by greed".

Nobody came out of the documentary well. Miss Australia accused Julia of ruthlessly extracting money from developing nations – Nigeria had paid a fee of £5m for the rights to stage Miss World – while Miss England, Daniella Luan, alleged that she was so reluctant to gain from the whole affair that she had hatched a plot with Julia to stay on as a contestant only if the judges agreed not to vote for her.

The documentary also alleged that Miss Turkey won only because she was a Muslim, and that the contestants were treated like babies and were totally under the control of the organisation.

These slurs infuriated Julia. She rapidly issued a statement refuting the "disgraceful allegations, entirely untrue", and said she would be consulting lawyers.

She was also quick to slap down Miss England's claim by offering to produce the judges' voting cards showing their scores for her and that "she didn't make the top 20 even in the public internet vote".

At least the new Miss World took her beleaguered boss's side. "People who think Miss World is to blame should research more about this competition", said Azra Akin. "We are doing great things".

Azra certainly managed to do great things for herself. She took part in Channel 4's mini-Olympics for celebrities, *The Games*, and on the way to winning the Gold Medal, she put Spice Girl Mel C (Sporty) in hospital with a ruptured knee ligament during a Judo match.

Journalist Isioma Daniel fled into exile as a political refugee and today lives in Norway.

In an article for the Canadian Broadcasting Company, reflecting on those tumultuous events in Nigeria, she wrote, "Whatever happened to dialogue? Or letters to the Editor? Or peaceful demonstrations? Or good old fashioned office politics where I would have been re-deployed to the agriculture desk?

I am being naïve again."

Tara Conner

"I suffer from the disease of alcoholism and addiction"

Tara Conner, Miss USA 2006

Beauty contests took such a dip in popularity during the '90s that any whiff of a scandal or a misdemeanour didn't make it into the news anyway, even if they happened. Mainstream television in the UK resolutely refused to find a space in the schedules for the major pageants, leaving Miss World waving and quite possibly drowning in the satellite stations of obscurity.

It was only when a new millennium dawned that a strange thing happened. People started getting the bug again for beauty contests. Viewers, newly hooked on a relentless diet of reality shows that made stars out of nobodies, questioned whether beauty contests were actually much different.

And the young women themselves, brainwashed into believing that only a top notch career and perfect family would do for their future, suddenly saw the fun and opportunity that presented itself when they took part in a local heat for Miss Such-and-Such.

The reasons for entering beauty contests were almost identical as to those in the '60s. Women may have more career opportunities in the 21st century, but many still dallied with the idea of instant riches and that oh-so-desirable commodity of celebrity and their fifteen minutes of fame.

So we got the beauty contests back. All we needed was a decent scandal to go with it.

Step forward, please, Tara Elizabeth Conner, Miss USA 2006.

Stateside, Donald Trump owned The Miss Universe Organisation and was hellbent on taking his pageants back to their '70s heyday. Mindful of the fact that Julia Morley was still running his only major rival, the Miss World contest based in London, he made her several offers for a buy-out following her husband Eric's death in 2000, and was furious to be rebuked each time.

As a result, Julia was unable to get a foothold on the US market. She told *The Observer*: "Trump won't let me through the door. He's offered to buy me out, but he won't let me in."

Trump installs the winners of his three pageants, Miss USA, Miss Universe and Miss Teen USA, in a sumptuous apartment for their year of office in Trump Tower, and enforces strict rules – no swearing, drinking or smoking, either in public or inside the apartment.

In the history of the Miss USA pageant, which began in 1952, only one winner had ever been sacked, and that had been way back in 1957. Unlike their British counterparts, the all-American girls came across as saintly, sanitised, and sin-free.

So it came as a shocking – and refreshing – change when scandal hit 20 year old blonde Tara Conner, eight months after her crowning as Miss USA at the famous Kodak Theatre in Los Angeles.

The student had been competing in beauty pageants since the age of four, but her true crowning moment was in becoming the only woman from Kentucky to win the Miss USA crown. Part of her prize was to live in Trump's apartment with Miss Universe and Miss Teen USA as flatmates.

However, an obscure American website reported that all may not be well inside Trump Tower. There were rumours that Tara was about to be stripped of her crown following some unseemly behaviour.

Two days later, The *New York Daily News* went a step further. Tara had tested positive for cocaine, had kissed Miss Teen USA in public, and had sneaked men into their apartment.

One New York City nightlife veteran said, "She really is a small-town girl from Kentucky. She went wild when she came to the city. Tara just couldn't handle herself. They were sneaking those nightclub guys in and out of the apartment." According to Fox News, Tara had moved out of the apartment a few days after the story broke.

America held its breath – as did the Miss USA runner-up who was desperate to inherit the crown, if only for the remaining four months. Would Tara hear those words from her boss's other top rated TV show, *The Apprentice* – "You're fired"?

At an emotionally-charged press conference - held the day after Tara's 21st birthday and triggered as a result of her positive drugs test - Trump, milking the occasion for all it was worth - intoned, "I've always believed in second chances. Tara will stay on as Miss USA". He patted her heaving shoulders and smiled down at her benignly, aware that there wasn't a dry eye in the house.

Trump admitted that he had expected to dismiss Conner, "but after speaking to her I saw not only a beautiful woman, but a beautiful heart. She really, really tried."

As Tara sobbed her gratitude to her saviour and mentor, she vowed in front of the world's TV cameras to enter rehab and avenge her 'serious mistakes'. Turning to Trump, she said, "You'll never know what this means to me, and I swear I will not let you down."

After two months at the Caron Foundation Facility in Pennsylvania, Tara began a whirlwind of TV interview confessionals, promising that she'd faced her demons and hinting at a dark past involving abuse and anti-depressants.

She appeared on the *Today* show and admitted to cocaine abuse and a chaotic childhood. "I will not deny that I have witnessed some abuse, but out of respect for my family ... it's something I would like to speak with them about first," she stated.

Tara told *People* magazine that she felt like a "completely different person" since she left rehab. "Before I entered rehab I hardly knew who I was. I felt like I was floating and I just needed someone to pull me down.

"I suffer from the disease of alcoholism and addiction. And if there's anything that I want people to know it's the severity of this disease and what it can do to people."

In the US documentary series, *Fame and Recovery*, Tara explained how she had started drinking and taking prescription drugs at the age of 14 to mask her unhappiness over her parents' divorce and the death of her grandfather. Around the same time she says she was raped by a man and started self-harming to, as she put it, "controlling the pain and controlling the feelings".

She soon learned that winning a pageant meant her bad and erratic behaviour around her parents and at school was forgiven. Yet she was high on the biggest night of her life. "I was doing pain pills throughout the whole Miss USA pageant. So when they called my name, I just kind of covered my face. ... I think, 'This is what I'm supposed to do.' But I didn't even feel it."

After she won, Tara quickly realised that she didn't have the mental or emotional capacity to carry out her role. "I didn't even realise I was suffering from a disease that was literally taking me out lie by lie, manipulation by manipulation and drink by drink," she says.

When Donald Trump held the press conference to determine her future, Tara felt that even though she had asked him for a second chance, she would've been happy with either decision. "Part of me was like, 'Wow, all of my skeletons are out there,'" she says. "There's a freedom that comes with that."

After learning that Tara had been on drugs during the Miss USA competition, Trump admitted she would never have won the title if he had known at the time. "We didn't know about her drug use," he said. "Had we had an idea, she probably wouldn't even have been in the contest to start with."

From the beginning of Tara's reign, Trump says the Miss USA staff had wanted her out. Originally, he had planned on firing her, he told *People*, but after a meeting with her in his office, he had a change of heart. "I hated it from the concept of what it would do to somebody's life," he says. "I said I was going to give her a second chance. ... The biggest backlash I had was not from the public. I think the public liked it. The biggest backlash I had was from the staff."

Trump's own brother had died from alcoholism and his decision was undoubtedly swayed by this personal tragedy.

"I believe in second chances," he said. "Tara went from being a disaster to a terrific Miss USA. But, much more importantly, she sets an example for so many other people who are going through the same thing".

Tara handed over her Miss USA crown in April 2007 and signed a deal to write a book about her childhood and her life in rehab. She also won a role in the MTV reality series *Pageant Place*, as 'minder' to the three beauty queens who took up residence in Trump Tower after she and her fellow housemates moved out once their reigns were over.

Tara says she now loves the woman she has become. "Even if you don't love yourself at all, other people do love you," she told *Fame and Recovery*. "I've had so many people come forward and help me, and I've been so fortunate in my life. I don't feel I deserve any of the good things I got, but apparently I do. And through the course of other people loving me, I learned how to love myself."

She now helps raise awareness of addiction through the National Youth Recovery Foundation in the States, and recently celebrated six years of sobriety.

Donald Trump's good nature, though, had a limit. Just two days after handing Tara a reprieve, he sacked the reigning Miss Nevada USA, Katie Rees, when racy pictures of her simulating oral sex and kissing other women at a party surfaced.

Trump was proven correct in his judgment of Katie. In February 2008 she was pulled over by Las Vegas traffic police for speeding, whereupon they also discovered that she was driving with an invalid licence, invalid licence plates, and no insurance.

When stopped from being allowed to drive away, she began kicking out at one of the officers. She was arrested, taken to Clark County Detention Center and only released after twelve hours in custody. The charges were later dropped and Katie won a lawsuit against the Las Vegas metropolitan police department citing "excessive force" which had occurred during the same incident leaving her with a bruised, scraped and swollen arm and hip, a black eye and chin, and a missing front tooth.

Tara's poignant story and Katie's outrageous antics were seen as being single-handedly responsible for re-igniting interest in pageants Stateside.

All hail, the bad girls - Donald's trump card.

Rosanna Davison

"I don't get my looks from my Dad"

Rosanna Davison, Miss World 2003

When Rosanna Davison chose to wear a bright pink evening gown to the 2003 Miss World finals, she broke a thousand copywriters' hearts.

For the gorgeous Miss Ireland was the daughter of singer Chris de Burgh, whose biggest hit was the legendary *Lady in Red*.

The Independent newspaper was so desperate to include the connection when reporting that Rosanna had won Miss World, they alluded to the crimson-attired runner-up from China and came up with the clumsy headline, "Miss Ireland upstages lady in red".

The press had been highly amused throughout the competition that Chris de Burgh – with the kind of looks that were never likely to adorn many posters – had produced such a stunningly beautiful daughter. Even Rosanna admitted, "I don't know where I got my looks from. But I definitely don't take after my dad".

Rosanna was the type of willowy blonde for whom the Miss World crown was made. She had been the hot favourite to triumph all along, and nobody was surprised when she gave Ireland its first victory (again, optimistically reported in the press as being a 'victory for the British Isles').

Her crowning also gave the Miss World organisation its best press for years and a great deal of it too – the story made front page news in most of the UK newspapers and this time not due to riots or protests.

So it was hardly surprising that one faction felt it a little too convenient that the daughter of a worldwide star had won the contest. Rosanna's shocking pink frock had hardly been packed away before the dissenters became vocal.

It was alleged that her famous father's friendships with some of the judges had tipped the scales in Rosanna's favour. Entertainer Bruce Forsyth, known to be close to the de Burgh family, was involved in earlier rounds of the Miss World contest, while his wife, Wilnelia, Miss World 1975, was on the judging panel when Rosanna won Miss Ireland.

Bookmakers had also reported a surge of big last-minute bets on her, making her the most heavily-backed contestant in history.

The Miss World PR juggernaut waded in. "There is no truth in it," said a spokesman. "Anyone can see why she won it. She is stunning, personable and amiable."

This was not a new accusation. When Rosanna won the Miss Ireland title in Dublin some months earlier, the press were out in force calling that a fix, too. One of the judges, pop supremo Louis Walsh, had allegedly told reporters before the contest had even started that Rosanna was going to win. Louis strenuously denied this.

One woman actually called out "Fix!" from the back of the room as Rosanna took her crown, and furthermore several newspapers believed it was such a foregone conclusion they'd already printed their articles reporting that she'd won.

Not surprisingly, this new round of allegations marred Rosanna's night of glory at the Miss World contest in Sanya, China. She said they were an "insult to the integrity of the judges".

Perhaps unwisely, she went on to slam 'small-minded' Ireland and its 'begrudgers' of her fame. "In Ireland people just can't accept other people's success", she said.

Rather than sidestepping any further influence from, or mention of, her famous father, Rosanna then ploughed into the murky waters of de Burgh's infamous affair with the family nanny, which had made headlines in 1994.

Maresa Morgan was 19 – the same age as Rosanna – when she embarked on an affair with the singer. The scandal was compounded by the fact that de Burgh's wife Diane was in hospital at the time, recovering from breaking her neck in a fall.

Rosanna was interviewed in the *Sunday Mirror* about the affair and could hardly have been more scathing. Maresa, she said, "disgusts me, she's pathetic. We trusted her and she was employed to look after us children. I hope she pays for it. To do such a dreadful thing at such an age is terrible".

She reserved none of her contempt for her father. "I never felt angry with Dad – he handled it well, explaining everything carefully".

As for the controversy that steeped her wins, she said. "It's jealousy, purely putting down people's achievements. I expected it in Ireland."

Any connection with Chris de Burgh may have been regretted by Julia Morley. Rosanna's reign wore on but, by March of the following year, she had yet to sign a formal contract with the organisation – on the advice of her father. This impasse meant that Rosanna's reign fell short of the usual whirlwind schedule of travel, meetings and promotions.

In shades of the Lesley Langley debacle, it was alleged that Rosanna had refused to attend functions arranged for her by the Miss World Organisation, and had instead arranged her own engagements. Her solicitors denied this, but did confirm that she had finally signed the re-negotiated contract – in June, halfway through her reign.

There was never any question of Rosanna being reprimanded for her stubbornness or indeed for her outbursts in the press, but Julia probably sighed with relief when she returned to China – this time dressed in red – to crown her successor.

Rosanna is now a big name in Irish celebrity circles and her name appears in the media almost as much as her father's. Among her many TV appearances in 2007 was as a competitor on *Celebrity Jigs 'n' Reels* (the equivalent to the UK's *Strictly Come Dancing*). She was the third person to be voted off.

Numerous TV appearances followed, from the *British Comedy Awards*, *GMTV, Come Dine With Me*, and even as a presenter on Liverpool FC's dedicated TV channel, *LFC TV*.

Yet her acceptance by the Irish public was neither easy nor immediate. The *Irish Mail on Sunday* ran an in-depth interview with her and criticised her "moral posture" and "inauthenticity", accusing her of an "indiscriminate rush for cash" in accepting any job offered to her, regardless of her beliefs or principles.

Her on-off relationship with 'slot machine' heir Wesley Quirke was another source of entertainment in Ireland, although it culminated in their engagement in 2013.

Rosanna hit the headlines again after a remark she made concerning Ryanair's 2009 charity calendar. She told a journalist, "If I was organising it, I would have made sure that Irish women were involved because it's an Irish charity and Irish fundraising."

The following day, the airline released a statement to the effect that Rosanna's remarks "bordered on racism and demonstrated an elitist attitude against Ryanair's international cabin crew".

Rosanna hit back and sued Ryanair for defamation of character, which she considered made her look racist, xenophobic and jealous.

In 2011 a jury awarded her a total of €80,000 (£68,000) for damages.

Ryanair's Head of Communications, Stephen McNamara, told journalists afterwards that it would be a "good outcome" if Ms Davison chose to give her award to the charity which had benefited from the calendar, but that it was for her to decide.

When asked if Irish girls would be represented in the 2012 calendar he said, in a barely-concealed aside, "Rosanna herself can apply. If she wants to apply we'll consider her, but the best girls will always get in."

Rosanna made history in 2013 by becoming the only Miss World to ever pose nude for the American version of *Playboy* magazine. The photos had first appeared in the German edition, with her father's blessing, and they had impressed boss Hugh Hefner so much that he invited her to meet him at his infamous Playboy Mansions for a private dinner with him and his new wife.

With her marriage to Wes planned for the summer of 2014, Rosanna has established herself as a regular face on Irish and British TV, as well as qualifying as a nutritionist, ensuring that this lady need never be in the red.

Danielle Lloyd

"They eat with their hands in India, don't they?"

Danielle Lloyd, Miss Great Britain 2006

D anielle Lloyd's defining achievement was to turn the clock back to the '70s. In an age in which beauty queens were trying hard to appear intelligent, modern and career-orientated, she dated one of the judges - who was also a famous footballer - posed topless, and got sacked. If you were to write a script full of beauty queen clichés, you could do worse than follow Danielle's career.

The modern twist, though, was the advent of reality TV. Whereas three decades ago the shamed beauty queen would turn up full frontal in all the top shelf publications, or marry a minor singer or businessman, Danielle cashed in on her notoriety in the most public – and disastrous – way possible: *Celebrity Big Brother*.

But before we get ahead of ourselves, let's rewind the tape and find ourselves in Bournemouth, where pretty Liverpudlian lass Danielle Lloyd is crowned Miss England 2004. She wasn't the most beautiful contestant, nor the most personable (she dried up completely during her on-stage interview) but she possessed that *je ne sais quoi* that gave her the winning edge.

A trip to China for the Miss World finals beckoned and although she didn't come close to winning, Danielle proved herself to be an enthusiastic and respectable ambassador for England.

And there her story may have ended had she not, on a whim, decided to enter the Miss Great Britain contest in January 2006. It was a high risk strategy – a former Miss World contestant opening herself up to being beaten. But it paid off – she was chosen the winner by an eclectic mix of judges, including racing pundit John McCririck, ex-jailbird Lord Charlie Brockett, Sven Goran-Eriksson's femme fatale Faria Alam....and West Ham and England footballer Teddy Sheringham.

Her reign proceeded swimmingly. She got together with Teddy, she said, at the party after the contest, and they were featured in the glossy magazines as the new celebrity couple. Never mind that she was nearly the same age as Teddy's daughter – becoming a WAG was the ultimate achievement for the likes of Danielle and her ilk.

She also made a memorable appearance on BBC1's *Test the Nation*. She was asked: "Who was Winston Churchill - a rapper, a US President, a Prime Minister or a King?" Danielle answered "Wasn't he the first black president of America? There's a statue of him near me - that's black."

Then came that fatal interview with *Eve* magazine in September. "Teddy got me this amazing pair of £7,000 Jimmy Choo shoes for Christmas," she gushed. "I was there in my pyjamas in the bedroom, in these heels, strutting up and down the carpet".

Christmas? But Danielle only met Teddy in January, didn't she, on the night he judged her in the contest? The cat was well and truly out of the bag – they had obviously been canoodling well before Teddy's vote had helped Danielle to title.

The Miss Great Britain Organisation swung into action and fired her without delay.

Danielle protested her innocence, saying that the magazine had misquoted her, and she had "only been trying to be helpful".

At the same time, *Playboy* magazine was trumpeting on its website the topless debut of Miss Great Britain 2006, despite the rules stating quite clearly that any nude photo shoots during her reign are forbidden. It was the 1970s all over again.

The Miss Great Britain Organisation appeared to take an almost sadistic pleasure in announcing the sacking of Danielle. On their website it proudly proclaimed that, "News of her sacking has made front pages all over the world, including the *New York Post*".

"Miss Cheat Britain", screamed the headlines. Danielle was distraught. But not for long. Who better to take part in Endemol's *Celebrity Big Brother* TV show than a disgraced beauty queen and WAG? Here was her chance of redemption, alongside a host of failed pop stars and D-listers.

If becoming a household name was Danielle's aim, she succeeded admirably. Along with fellow housemates Jade Goody and Jo O'Meara, Danielle attracted negative publicity on a worldwide scale over the racist bullying of Bollywood actress Shilpa Shetty in the Big Brother house.

Shilpa, Danielle was heard to say during the programme, was "a dog", and should "f**k off home".

"They eat with their hands in India don't they?" she asked her fellow housemates. "Or is that China? You don't know where her hands have been".

Her remarks, and those of Goody and O'Meara, made the TV news and headlines all over the world.

Danielle had talked to the press a great deal before going into the Big Brother house about her own experiences as the victim of a bully at school, as well as the abuse she suffered at the hands of a violent ex-boyfriend. She had also fronted an anti-bullying campaign.

Once her own bullying tendencies were exposed on national TV, her former headmaster in Liverpool spoke out to put the record straight.

In the *Daily Record* newspaper, St Hilda's Church of England High School head Chris Yates said, "I've looked at Danielle's school record and spoken to former year heads. There is no recollection of her ever being persecuted and no teacher can ever recall any incidents where Danielle was bullied.

"In fact, I've been led to believe by her former friends that, if anything, the opposite was true.

"Danielle's conduct on *Big Brother* reflects very badly on her. It is a shame that one unremarkable pupil, who has achieved minor celebrity in one form or another, has cast a shadow over our remarkable school."

Twisting the knife, Mr Yates also poured scorn on Danielle's televised claims that she was a top student. He went on: "Danielle has over-inflated the quality of her qualifications. She left St Hilda's because the GCSE grades she received would not have been sufficient for her to go on and take A-Levels."

Thousands of complaints about the bullying on *Celebrity Big Brother* were filed with Ofcam and even soon-to-be Prime Minister Gordon Brown spoke out to condemn the show.

In the only acceptable result, Shilpa Shetty won the final, while it looked as though Danielle's career was over. Teddy dumped her – he cited the mass of publicity that he couldn't cope with – and several of her lucrative modelling contracts were cancelled.

The Miss Great Britain organisation crowed with delight on their website. "With hindsight it would have been better not to have fired Danielle last November because we could have fired her today and if we could fire her twice we would!!"

Determined to clear her name on at least one front, she sued the Miss GB organisation for libel, and she was finally cleared of cheating in the competition, after Teddy had signed a statement saying that they had met after the contest.

Danielle also publicly made friends with Shilpa Shetty at the Leicester Square premiere of the actress's new film. The two ex-housemates hugged on the red carpet and the flashbulbs went wild.

"I think I was naive in what I did in the house," she told the *Liverpool Echo*. "It was like a bunch of schoolkids in there; little bitchy schoolgirls."

In November 2007 she received "substantial damages" from the *Daily Mirror* over allegations that she had had a two hour sex session in a nightclub changing room with rapper 50 Cent and that she had propositioned That Take singer Jason Orange, while she was dating footballer Marcus Bent.

"I think if I'd let them get away with that then they'd have taken the p*** for the rest of my life," she said of the legal action. "I couldn't let that happen, especially when I saw my mum and my nan crying. I don't want people to think I'm the sort of girl who goes and sleeps with anyone because that just isn't true. But even now they say I'm seeing Tom, Dick and Harry every week."

The serial WAG then hooked up with yet another footballer, Spurs striker Jermain Defoe. Defoe had only recently dumped fiancée Charlotte Mears, who until that point had been a good friend of Danielle's. The relationship lasted two months before Defoe took Charlotte back.

Despite such trials, tribulations, and backlash, there was no keeping the lass from Penny Lane down. Proving her many detractors wrong, she won a celebrity edition of TV quiz show *The Weakest Link*, fought her way to victory in the physically demanding final of *Celebrity Total Wipeout*, and competed in Tom Daley's Saturday night TV diving competition, *Splash!*

She also released a fitness DVD called *Keep Fit, Look Fit*, which became an instant bestseller.

Her greatest vindication, however, came at the start of 2010. The new owners of the Miss Great Britain brand declared that, due to the lack of guidance and poor management of Danielle when she won her crown four years earlier, it had been an unfair decision to sack her when she posed for *Playboy* magazine. To that end, they said, she would be reinstated as the officially-named titleholder on their website.

Therefore on both levels – the accusation of cheating, and the nude modelling - Danielle had finally cleared her name. Despite the traumas at the time, she was canny enough to know that, but for her very public dethroning and the resultant publicity, she would've had to take a very different route in order to achieve household name status.

In December 2009, she announced her engagement to Portsmouth FC midfielder Jamie O'Hara. They married in 2012 and now have three sons.

One beauty contest contemporary of Danielle's, who prefers to remain anonymous, said, "Say what you like about Danielle – she's a modern day role model for young women. She lived the dream – Miss World, footballers, TV fame, magazine covers. This is why so many women still want to be beauty queens, for the very lifestyle that Danielle has achieved. Don't get me wrong, there are still girls in it for the glamour and for a laugh, but many see it as a fast-track to stardom, and Danielle has set the standard.

"Don't be fooled by those who say they want to win so they can help starving children and achieve world peace.

"Deep down, they really want to be like Danielle."

Vanessa Williams

"I am not a lesbian and I am not a slut"

Vanessa Williams, Miss America 1984

When Vanessa's music teacher parents wrote: "Here she is: Miss America", on their daughter's birth certificate, they had no idea how prophetic that statement would be. Nor could they ever have predicted the resulting fall-out.

Vanessa was only persuaded by pageant scouts to compete in the Syracuse heat of the Miss New York pageant because her university campus musical, in which she was starring, was cancelled. As the Miss New York winner, Vanessa made history by becoming the first ever African-American to win the Miss America title in September 1983.

The significance of this win simply couldn't be overestimated. The pageant, which has been held since 1921, and which has no affiliation with either the Miss Universe or Miss World organisations, banned non-white women from competing for many years. "Rule number seven" of their entry form stated that: "Contestants must be of good health and of the white race". Black women were allowed to appear in the show's musical numbers, but usually cast as slaves.

Indeed, until at least 1940, contestants were required to complete a questionnaire tracing their ancestry. It was as late as 1970 that the first African-American contestant took part in the pageant.

But for twenty year old Vanessa, it was an easy victory in 1983. She'd already won the preliminary competitions in Swimsuit and, significantly, Talent, with a stunning rendition of Barbra Streisand's *Happy Days Are Here Again*.

The runner-up, Suzette Charles, Miss New Jersey, was also of African-American descent, the first and, to date, only time that the top two spots have been taken by women of colour.

Speaking to a local Arizona newspaper a decade later, Vanessa said, "It was never a crown I coveted. From childhood, my goal was performing. Which made the nightmare that followed my becoming Miss America all the more ironic".

She became the first Miss America to receive hate mail, demanding to know how she could be labelled as a true African-American, when her Caucasian heritage had clearly blessed her with dark blonde hair and blue eyes.

Vanessa told a magazine reporter that she was confused too. "Growing up in a predominantly white, middle-class environment, I thought I was just like everyone else. When I won Miss America, that's when reality set in. I got hate mail from white-supremacist groups and also from blacks who didn't feel I was black enough. I didn't know who I was: she's black, she's not black enough, she's not white so we hate her."

But support came from unexpected quarters. President Ronald Reagan phoned her in Atlantic City straight after her win. "Congratulations, Vanessa. This is a great thing for our nation."

Ten months into her reign as Miss America, she received an anonymous phone call informing her that nude photographs of her, posing explicitly with another woman, had surfaced. These had been taken by a photographer two years previously, and Vanessa had been led to believe that they were not only private, but had also been destroyed. She claimed never to have signed a release allowing them to be used in any form.

The photographs were originally offered to Hugh Hefner, the publisher of *Playboy*. He turned them down immediately, and in a subsequent magazine interview explained why. "They clearly weren't authorised," he said, "and because they would be a source of considerable embarrassment to her, we decided not to publish them".

He added, "We were also mindful that she was the first black Miss America".

Bob Guccione, of *Penthouse*, wasn't so circumspect. He snapped them up and printed them in the September 1984 issue. The cover photo showed Vanessa next to comedian George Burns and the headline, 'Miss America, Oh God, She's Nude!'

The publication of the pictures set off a media frenzy. After several pageant sponsors threatened to pull out of the forthcoming 1985 contest, Vanessa came under heavy pressure by Miss America officials to resign.

Vanessa was an extremely popular Miss America and the country stood firmly behind her in her hour of need. Well-wishers filled her parents' New York home with flowers, telegrams and letters of encouragement, urging her to fight to keep her crown.

Outside the hotel hosting the televised press conference in which she would announce her decision, supporters carried placards reading, "We love you Vanessa and will always respect you".

When she stepped forward to confirm that she had decided to renounce the title – "It is not my desire to injure in any way the Miss America title or pageant" - even the assembled reporters groaned in sympathy.

Vanessa handed over the title to her runner-up, Suzette Charles, who took over for the last seven weeks of the reign. Vanessa was allowed to keep her bejewelled crown and scholarship money, and The Miss

America Organisation still officially recognises her as Miss America 1984, with Suzette listed as Miss America 1984-B.

She wasn't though, prepared to walk off the world's stage quietly. "I am not a lesbian and I am not a slut," she declared to *People* Magazine. "Somehow I am going to make people believe me."

Her immediate future was bleak. Vanessa decided against returning to school, but any acting roles offered came mainly from the adult entertainment industry, while record companies were reluctant to embrace her less-than-wholesome image.

The tabloids nicknamed her, 'Vanessa the Undressa'. One Baltimore columnist wrote, "Vanessa Williams is not going anywhere in the entertainment world; she doesn't have the talent."

In her 2012 autobiography, *You Have No Idea*, Vanessa writes: "For me, it seemed like an eternity in which I was the punchline to every late-night monologue. Joan Rivers was particularly relentless. Just when I'd figured she'd exhausted every possible Vanessa Williams joke, she'd have a whole new slew of them."

She filed a lawsuit against the photographer who sold the nude pictures but eventually decided not to pursue it, saying, "The best revenge is success".

And revenge, for Vanessa, couldn't have come any sweeter. With the guidance of PR expert Ramon Hervey (who became her first husband), she went on to lead what is arguably the most successful career of any former Miss America – indeed, of any pageant winner in history – releasing no fewer than eight hit albums since 1988, and scoring a massive worldwide smash with the single, *Save the Best for Last*.

To date, she has sold over six million records and received eleven Grammy Award nominations, as well as award-winning appearances in plays, TV shows, Broadway musicals and films, most notably alongside Miley Cyrus in *Hannah Montana: The Movie*. The song she performed on the *Pocahontas* soundtrack, *Colors of the Wind*, won the Academy Award for Best Original Song in 1995.

Vanessa's big TV break came when she landed the role of bitchy fashionista Wilhelmina Slater in the worldwide smash sitcom, *Ugly Betty*, for which she was nominated three times for an Emmy award.

She joined the cast of *Desperate Housewives* for the sixth season and is currently starring in the ABC Television supernatural drama *666 Park Avenue*.

A twice-married and divorced mother of four, Vanessa received a Star on the Hollywood Walk of Fame in 2007, to celebrate her twenty years in the entertainment industry, while in the same year posing nude for *Allure* magazine.

Her autobiography also revealed, for the first time, the abuse she suffered as a 10 year old child at the hands of an 18 year old daughter of a family friend, as well as her rebellious teen years in which she smoked marijuana and had an abortion in her senior year.

When Nina Davuluri was crowned the first Indian-American Miss America in 2013 – also, coincidentally, competing as Miss New York - she too faced a backlash of xenophobic and racist comments from certain sections of the public, but took great strength and inspiration from Vanessa's subsequent success.

Thirty years on from making history in Atlantic City, Vanessa was back in the resort performing for a sell-out crowd at Caesars Casino. "It all started here," she told her audience. "You've been with me from the very beginning – ups and downs."

Three decades on and, for the only Miss America in history to relinquish her crown, Vanessa's revenge gets sweeter by the day.

Imogen Thomas

"I've been hung out to dry"

Imogen Thomas, Miss Wales 2003

If Marjorie Wallace fell foul of a footballer, and Danielle Lloyd was felled by Big Brother, it was surely only a matter of time before a beauty queen's association with both common denominators would lead to our most recent Misdemeanour, and one of the most far-reaching.

Her liaison with one of the world's best-known sportsmen led to what one newspaper called "one of the biggest communal acts of civil disobedience of all time", and was even discussed in the House of Commons and at the G8 summit.

Imogen Thomas was 21 when she was crowned Miss Wales 2003, and went on to represent the principality at the Miss World contest in China. She was unplaced but returned home determined to seek a career in the bright lights of London.

Three years later, she was selected as a housemate for the seventh series of Channel 4's *Big Brother*, where she proved a popular contestant and resisted eviction until Day 86. She was later that year voted the sexiest housemate of all time.

A modest career as a minor celebrity ensued, and Imogen chose to tread the well-worn path of topless photo shoots for lads' mags and glamour calendars, supplemented with appearances at parties and events in London, dating footballers Matthew Collins and Jermain Defoe, as well as a brief liaison with Russell Brand.

Imogen briefly hit the headlines of the tabloid press in 2009, when she was diagnosed with swine flu following a holiday in Marbella.

So far, so unremarkable. Until April 2011, when she came became, briefly, the most infamous woman in the world.

The Sun initially broke the news of "Footie Star's Affair with Big Bro Imogen". They met at luxury hotels, it was alleged, before key matches, and Imogen was spotted leaving the player's room.

The first paragraph reads, "A Premier League star last night gagged *The Sun* after we found him romping with busty *Big Brother* babe Imogen Thomas behind his wife's back."

Imogen was photographed the next morning in tears at having been exposed as the mistress and was reported to have been devastated at the ending of the fling. As friends rallied round, they told reporters that she had been convinced he would leave his wife and children for her. "She said that he told her she was the love of his life," said one. "We thought he was going to propose. She was one hundred percent certain that he would leave his wife for her."

The footballer's agent was genuinely shocked when told of the story. "This is incredible. I can't believe it," he said. "He's such a family man."

The legal restriction placed on *The Sun* was soon followed by the serving of a super-injunction, a controversial piece of legislation prohibiting the press from reporting on even the existence of an injunction, or any of its details. A spate of super-injunctions had emerged that spring, from desperate high-profile figures rich enough to pay the £50,000 required to keep their names and misdemeanours out of the newspapers.

The footballer in question instructed his lawyers to press ahead with this super-injunction which, at its most draconian, could send to jail anyone who revealed his name in relation to the affair.

Imogen Thomas was, to all intents and purposes, left to face the lion's den of the media. She appeared on breakfast TV in tears, complaining that she had been "hung out to dry" while her former lover could hide behind the protection of the gagging order.

"I had no intention of selling my story," she sobbed to Philip Schofield. In fact, this is exactly what she had done, telling a breathless account – through PR guru Max Clifford - of the affair to a Sunday tabloid, though being forced, of course, to omit her lover's name.

They had met at a London club and the couple found that they had so much in common that they retired to his hotel straight away. "Back at the hotel bar we were just chatting about life, but I could tell he was interested in me. We kissed and I ended up staying the night."

They continued to meet over the next six months despite, said Imogen, her attempts to call it off several times. "He knew it was wrong as well, he said as much, but he was pursuing me."

Such is the power of the internet that by this time the footballer's name was becoming widely known to the public, via social networking sites such as Twitter and Facebook, and was being discussed in detail in chatrooms and online forums.

The name that came up again and again was that of Ryan Giggs, the 37 year old Manchester United player and one of the most respected men in football. The former BBC Sports Personality of the Year was a renowned family man, husband and father of two. In a world where every other footballer was seemingly cheating, lying and deceiving, Giggs was seen as the decent face of the game.

But no longer, it would seem. Imogen was back in front of the TV cameras again a few days later, when a court upheld the gagging order due to strong evidence that she had attempted to 'blackmail' the footballer and that he had been 'set up'.

According to the footballer's witness statement, their last liaison had taken place in December, and he next heard from the model in March when she texted him to say she was considering selling her story.

She allegedly told the player she "needed £50,000". He agreed to meet her at a hotel and said that he was not prepared to pay her the money, but handed over a signed football shirt instead. She apparently contacted him again a few days later, and they met again, when he gave her some football tickets.

Finally, Imogen was said by the player to have contacted him once more 'making it clear that she was looking for £100,000".

The Judge presiding over the case pronounced that he had no choice but to uphold the super-injunction.

Imogen reacted with fury once again to these latest accusations and threatened to expose the identity of her former lover. "Yet again, my name and my reputation is being trashed while the man I had a relationship with is able to hide. I am tempted to say it is *this* person."

The furore that the super-injunction caused forced the Justice Secretary, Kenneth Clarke, into ordering an immediate review of how to instruct judges in future over the granting of gagging orders.

With speculation at fever pitch, a YouGov poll revealed that 72% of respondees knew who the rogue player was. With Giggs's name appearing on Twitter at the rate of, at one stage, 160 times a minute, the player made one last desperate attempt to protect his identity: he sued the website over allowing its members to mention his name.

It was too late, though. During the last weekend of the Premiership football season, crowds chanted his name before the televised match, and not even an appearance with his two children on the pitch to celebrate Manchester United's Premiership title win could quell the wildfire of certainty that now surrounded him.

Scotland, not covered by the gagging order law, published a thinly veiled photo of Giggs on the front cover of its *Sunday Herald* newspaper, leaving those north of the border with no more room for doubt.

The final nail in the coffin was delivered by LibDem MP John Hemming a day later. He used his Parliamentary Privilege – a legal immunity which protects against civil or criminal liability – to name Ryan Giggs during a House of Commons debate on privacy laws.

Within seconds, the news hit the global airwaves and Ryan's game was over. Every news bulletin led on the story and the next day's front pages were adorned with pictures of Giggs and Imogen and headlines such as, "Naming Ryan's Privates".

Yet, farcically, the High Court still refused to lift the gagging order, meaning that Giggs could be named only in relation to the report about John Hemming, and not in any other context. The judge asked, "Should the court buckle every time one of its orders meets widespread disobedience or defiance?"

Four TV personalities, including Piers Morgan and Boy George, were told they would face prosecution for 'outing' Ryan Giggs on Twitter, while cheated wife Stacey was seen leaving their marital home without her wedding ring.

Imogen, meanwhile, told the tabloids how she was drinking far too much to cope with the stress, and her sister revealed that she was on medication as a result of the blackmail allegations held against her in court. She still managed to meet with Max Clifford in a series of ever-shorter dresses, though, to "discuss her next move".

The affair was even discussed by world leaders at the G8 summit in France, as an example of the legal dilemmas thrown up by the internet.

But, for Giggs, the worst was far from over. A week later, his sister in law Natasha told the *News of the World* that she and the footballer had been enjoying an affair for the past eight years. Such was her outrage at learning that he had cheated on her with Imogen, she felt she had to speak out.

Giggs, she said, had met her for sex the day after the birth of both his children, and had continued until just a few months hence.

"When I found out he was cheating with Imogen too, I was really hurt," she told the paper through a 'friend'.

"I know that sounds really strange, but he wasn't just cheating on Stacey, he was cheating on me too. Our relationship was just about sex to him."

Giggs's wife Stacey staunchly stood by her man, despite such humiliating allegations, while Natasha compounded her ex lover's fury by following in her erstwhile rivals footsteps and appearing in the 2012 edition of *Celebrity Big Brother*.

Despite dire warnings in the media that Giggs's career and lucrative sponsorship deals were over, he continued to play as a regular member of the Manchester United squad, and that October was voted the first British winner of the international Golden Foot award, in recognition of his achievements on the pitch.

Imogen, meanwhile, was cleared by the High Court in December of any attempt or intention to blackmail Giggs, and she gave a series of interviews expressing her great relief and desire to move on.

"I will never have an affair again," she insisted. "Absolutely not. What I did was wrong. But there are only so many times you can say sorry."

In February 2013, Imogen gave birth to daughter Ariana, by Australian boyfriend Adam Horsley, while Natasha Giggs filed for divorce from her husband Rhodri two months later.

Imogen's PR guru, Max Clifford – whose clients also included the Miss World Organisation – was jailed for eight years in May 2014 on eight counts of assault on young women and girls dating from 1966-1985, following a successful prosecution under the police investigation Operation Yewtree.

Rachel Christie

"Black people should stop behaving in a way that stereotypes them"

Rachel Christie, Miss England 2009

Hers was a tough upbringing with a fairytale narrative – the sink estate niece of Olympic champion Linford Christie, crowned the first black Miss England. Here was her chance, she said, to show black kids that they could be whatever they wanted to be.

"Black people should stop behaving in a way that stereotypes them," she declared after her win. "That's my main focus in winning Miss England." She was also training for the 2012 London Olympics and appeared to be the perfect role model for a generation.

Three months after such a positive and inspirational interview in the *Daily Mail*, Rachel's dream was over – sacked as Miss England following an assault on a fellow beauty queen in a nightclub, with more disgrace to follow.

Rachel Sophia Adina Christie was born in a West London sink estate to Russell, brother of Linford, and Diana, a white Irish Catholic woman.

Russell was two years younger than Linford, both born in London to their Jamaican parents. The brothers were both blessed with sporting ability, but while Linford rose to worldwide fame as a result of his success, Russell chose instead to ignore his own talent, routinely finding himself in trouble with the law.

As Linford became captain of Great Britain's men's athletics team in 1989, his brother was starting a three-year jail sentence for attacking a former lover with a baseball bat.

Five years later he was sentenced to three and a half years for theft, and for the beating of another girlfriend.

Rachel remembers visiting her father at Parkhurst Prison on the Isle of Wight. "I can still see those massive black gates. It looked like the entrance to a dungeon," she says, adding, "He was a good man, devoted to us kids".

She also discovered she had a half-sister, born to a different mother, when she was six years old. But the biggest shock of Rachel's young life came just two years later when, worried at her husband's absence, her mother Diana rang the police, only to discover that he had been stabbed to death in the street over a drugs brawl.

Despite her tender age, Rachel sunk into what she recognises now as depression. "But I had to overcome it myself and build up my strength and confidence".

Diana – pregnant at that time with her fourth child - moved the family out of the rough estate and into a council house in West Kensington, making huge sacrifices to provide for her children.

Rachel attended an all-girl convent school in Camden, and life was tough. She was bullied for being skinny and lacking shape, but wasn't once tempted to try the drugs seemingly so easily available there. "God no," she said, aghast, "my big brother would've killed me".

After qualifying as a fitness instructor, she took up training at the age of 19 for the 400m and heptathlon, at the stadium named after her famous uncle in West London. Linford mentored her to push herself ever harder and her sights at the time of her winning Miss England were set on qualifying for the 2012 Olympic Games in London.

Despite being scouted on several occasions, Rachel had resisting the modelling route, until she decided to compete in the London heat of the Miss England contest to help fund her training. She won easily, and a month later became the first black Miss England in the history of the event.

"My dad would've been thrilled to see me win Miss England," she said poignantly.

Her aim next, she added, was to win Miss World, and then an Olympic gold. The media went mad over the choice of such a newsworthy winner. Miss England organiser Angie Beasley had hit the jackpot, it seemed, in securing maximum publicity for both Rachel and the profile of the contest.

However, Rachel's next appearance in the newspapers – in November, just days before she was due to fly to South Africa for the Miss World contest - wasn't part of the fairytale script.

On a date with her new boyfriend, David McIntosh – a Royal Marine, but better known as Tornado on Sky TV's *Gladiators* game show – she was ill-advised in the first place to attend a 'porn-themed' party at The Mansion Club in Manchester.

Dressed in pink as an angel, Rachel was approached by another guest, the reigning Miss Manchester, Sara Beverley Jones. The 21 year old blonde, a one-time extra on the TV soap *Hollyoaks*, was dressed in cavegirl outfit and began talking to Rachel about her relationship with David.

Sara Beverley was an ex-girlfriend of the Gladiator, and apparently showed Rachel risqué text messages that he had recently sent to her. An altercation between the two women followed, and fellow clubbers watched as Rachel hit Sara in the face and sent her tumbling to the floor.

Manchester Police were called to the club, and Sara was taken to hospital where she received treatment for superficial facial injuries.

Rachel was arrested on suspicion of assault, and released on bail until the following January.

It was clear straight away that there was no way that Rachel could continue as Miss England. After a hurriedly-arranged meeting with

Angie Beasley, the Miss England website announced that, "Due to the media attention following the allegations against her, Rachel Christie has now decided to withdraw from the Miss World competition and relinquish her Miss England crown.

"Rachel will concentrate on clearing her name and focus on training for the 2012 Olympics until this case is resolved."

Meanwhile, in a barracks in Surrey, Corporal Katrina Hodge received a phone call that would change her life forever. Could she, as runner up to Miss England, possibly organise time off from her army duties to fly out to South Africa for the Miss World contest?

The 22 year old known to her military colleagues as 'Combat Barbie' didn't hesitate to answer the call to arms. Despite having just a few days to prepare for the contest, she rose to the challenge immediately with a last-minute shopping dash for swimwear and evening gowns.

In a heartfelt interview with the *Daily Mail*, Rachel admitted, "I'm just so angry and disappointed with myself. I let myself down, my family, all these people who had such high hopes."

Shedding light on what happened that fateful night, she explained that she had met David McIntosh and Sara Jones at an event in August, unaware that at that stage they were a couple. "Sara came up to me and said, 'So how's Miss England?' and told me that we had competed in the same heats."

A month later, David contacted Rachel and asked her out. "A group of us went out in Manchester, and when we all got back to his house, my stuff had been thrown about and the word 'slag' scrawled on the wall in lipstick."

"David knew it was Sara. He called the police but didn't press charges. That's the first I knew that they had been together. She obviously liked him more than he liked her."

Rachel continued, "I started getting creepy texts from her, and when I saw her in the club that night I tried to keep my distance, but she came up to me and took my glass from me – it was threatening behaviour. It was just a commotion after that.

"I'd hate to think that people will think, 'like father like daughter,'" she said.

"I couldn't face my family after I was arrested," she added. "I stayed in Manchester for two weeks. I was so ashamed. It is hard but I have to come back from this. There must be something I can do to make my family proud again."

That day seemed rather far away. Two months later, in February, the car she was driving with boyfriend David as a passenger was stopped by police after it was seen to be without insurance. The policeman was immediately hit by a strong smell of alcohol and asked Rachel to provide a breath specimen.

She failed thirteen times to blow into the testing machine properly. The one test she was able to provide quickly showed she was over the drink-drive limit. At Paddington Green police station she was found to be fully insured to drive the car, yet was arrested for failing to provide a second specimen.

When the case went to court in July 2010, Rachel failed to make an appearance, and a warrant was issued for her arrest. After a week on the run, she handed herself in to the police, but not before losing a lucrative sponsorship deal with Renault who had provided her with her car.

No charges were eventually brought for either that offence or the assault on Miss Manchester, but she faced a twelve-month driving ban when the case reached court again. To add to her woes, doctors found a cyst on her ovaries that prevented her from continuing her training and therefore putting an end to her Olympics dream.

She also tried, unsuccessfully, to win a place in the *Big Brother* house.

There was, however, a ray of light in the sad and sorry decline of Rachel's life since she had won and lost the Miss England crown – a month after her failure to attend court, she found out she was pregnant with David's child, a baby boy named Logan, now aged three.

But the couple parted company on Boxing Day 2013 and David was shortly seen dating actress Kelly Brook.

Rachel wasn't impressed. "He likes girls with fake tits and Botox. Kelly is too plain and not glamorous enough for him. I know 100 per cent she is not David's type", she told *The Sun*, adding, "Even I wasn't David's type!

"He's very arrogant and loves publicity. He will wear tiny shorts in the freezing cold, just for attention. He would go out in a thong if he could. I really feel sorry for Kelly", she continued. She also claimed that David had proposed to her on four occasions despite their frequent arguments.

The model and Gladiator split up after just six weeks and Rachel told the *Daily Star* that Kelly had had a "lucky escape".

"I knew it wouldn't last," she said. "I said he was using her but people just said I was jealous. I heard they split because he was tipping off the press about their whereabouts, which is appalling."

Rachel also revealed that the courts had handed David a non-molestation order a month earlier to keep him away from their son, after she had sought protection following the blazing row and split on Boxing Day.

So when Kelly and David got back together and announced their engagement a month later, nobody was more shocked – and cynical – than Rachel.

However, despite a turbulent personal life, six months earlier, in July 2013, Rachel had at last been given the opportunity to compete in an international beauty pageant after the disappointment of stepping aside from Miss World. She won the title of Miss Supranational UK and travelled to Belarus for the worldwide final against 82 other contestants.

She didn't win, but for Rachel, it was a redemption of sorts and, in her joy at the prospect of a full year's reign, tweeted, "Happy I've been given another chance. This time I will do England proud!"